New Testament Survey

The Faith Unfurled

New Testament Survey:
The Faith Unfurled

14 audio Lessons plus
Supplementary Materials
and Examinations

Copyright © 2018 by Douglas Jacoby and Illumination Publishers.
   Original edition printed in 2005.
   ISBN: 978-0-9767583-1-0.
   All rights reserved. No part of this book may be duplicated, copied, translated, reproduced or stored mechanically or electronically without the specific, written permission of Douglas Jacoby and Illumination Publishers International.
   Printed in the United States of America.
   All scripture quotations, unless otherwise indicated, are taken from the NEW INTERNATIONAL VERSION. Copyright ©1973, 1978, 1984, 2011 by the International Bible Society. Used by permission of Zondervan Publishing House. All rights reserved.
   The "NIV" and "New International Version" trademarks are registered in the United States Patent Trademark Office by the International Bible Society. Use of either trademark requires the permission of the International Bible Society.
      Interior layout and cover design by Toney C. Mulhollan.
   Illumination Publishers titles may be purchased in bulk for classroom instruction, teaching seminars, or sales promotional use. For information, please email paul.ipibooks@me.com.
   Illumination Publishers cares deeply about using renewable resources and uses recycled paper whenever possible.

About the author: Since 2003 Dr. Douglas Jacoby has been a freelance teacher and consultant. With degrees from Duke, Harvard, and Drew, he has written over thirty books, recorded over 1000 podcasts, and spoken in numerous cities in over 150 nations around the world. Douglas is also Adjunct Professor of Bible and Theology at Lincoln Christian University.
For information about his work, speaking schedule, and teaching ministry, view his website at www.DouglasJacoby.com.

   There is a free ebook version for all purchases of the hard copy of this book available upon request. Go to www.ipibooks.com for details.

"The sea is dark and rough and cold,
    Yet other options have you not;
My servants, hale and stout and bold,
    Must venture forth, as well they ought.

"The tale once told now tell again—
    Nor, fearful, shrink back from the task;
They'll listen, and repent from sin;
    So quickly now do all I ask!

"The nations wait," said he, "so go!
    The message share in all the world;
Your canvas spread, on every sea,
    Make haste to sail—the faith unfurled."

—Douglas Jacoby

Table of Contents

I. Overview 7
    Introduction to The Faith Unfurled

II. Pax Romana 10
    Preparation for the First Coming

III. Jesus Christ 13
    The Life and Death of Jesus

IV. The Synoptic Gospels. 19
    Matthew, Mark, and Luke

V. The Fourth Gospel 22
    The Gospel of John

VI. Contradictions? 25
    Handling Bible Difficulties

VII. The First Generation. 34
    The book of Acts and how to read it

VIII. Paul I. 38
    The Life and Death of Paul

IX. Paul II 42
    Letters to churches and Paul's philosophy of missions

X. Paul III 45
    Letters to individuals, Pastoral Epistles,
    Church governance

XI. Hebrews. 51
    The two covenants, function of Hebrews,
    Jewish Christianity and the end of a generation

XII. The General Letters 57
    The epistles of James, Peter, John, and Jude

Table of Contents

XIII. Revelation. 61
    Reading apocalyptic literature; the end of the world

XIV. Conclusion. 65
    Unfurling the Faith!

Supplementary Materials

XV. New Testament Reading Tips. 68
    Getting the most out of your personal study

XVI. The Bible in a Year. 72
    A workable plan for reading the whole Bible

XVII. 100 Passages. 73
    Useful scriptures for teaching and counseling

XVIII. Dating. 77
    New Testament Chronology

XIX. Canon. 79
    How the New Testament came together

XX. New Testament Survey Class Series. 81
    Teaching *The Faith Unfurled* as a church course

XXI. New Testament Exams. 84
    At introductory, intermediate, and intensive levels

XXII. Resources. 97
    Helpful Books and Websites

New Testament Survey: The Faith Unfurled is the companion handbook to the audio series of the same name. Listen to the lessons as you follow along in the handbook. Extra space has been provided for notetaking purposes. For maximum learning benefit, keep your study Bible nearby and refer to it whenever an unfamiliar passage is cited. Let nothing slip by. For further study, consult the books and websites referenced in the bibliography at the end of the book as well as throughout the series. It is my hope and prayer that you will enjoy this survey series, and grow stronger in your Christian faith as a result.

— Douglas Jacoby

> But these are written that you may believe that Jesus is the Christ, the son of God, and that by believing you may have life in his name.
>
> – John 20:31

I

OVERVIEW
Introduction to The Faith Unfurled

> **Unfurl**
> v. 1641. **1.** *trans.* To spread (a sail or flag) to the wind. **B.** *transf.* To open (a fan, umbrella, etc.) 1678. *intr.* To open to the wind 1813.

I. What is this New Testament survey?

A. Not just a book about the New Testament

B. Not as focused as a commentary

C. Academic surveys focus on matters of lower and higher criticism

D. This survey has a more practical emphasis

   1. How to read the New Testament

   2. Identifying what God is trying to show us

II. Personal New Testament ownership!

A. We are fortunate to own personal copies of the New Testament

B. Printing Press (1400s) + Protestant Reformation (1500s) = personal Bible ownership

III. Extrabiblical reading

A. Read!

1. We need to become readers, even if this is not our natural inclination.

2. See bibliography (Chapter 22)

B. Building a library

1. What are your cultural values?

2. What books are in your home library?

IV. Reading the New Testament on five levels

A. Verses

1. Verse numbers added in 16th century

2. Useful New Testament Passages (see Chapter 17)

3. Challenge yourself!

B. Chapters

1. They are only headings—not the same as "chapters" in modern books.

2. Added in the Middle Ages

3. 260 in all

C. Books

1. Each has a theme. Ask, "Why is this book in the Bible?"

2. Grasp main idea of each New Testament book (see Chapter 15)

3. When reading a book of the Bible, get into the habit of reading it straight through.

D. Testament

1. Testament = covenant

2. The New Testament testifies to Jesus

3. "The Old Testament is the New Testament concealed; the New Testament is the Old Testament revealed."

4. There are many connections with the Old Testament
   a. Prophecy
   b. Themes and theology
   c. John the Baptist (Malachi 3-4)
   d. For more on this, see *Old Testament Survey: Foundations For Faith* (Illumination Publishers, 2004 [www.ipibooks.com])

E. The Bible
   1. The story of redemption—at God's initiative
   2. History as "his story"

V. Unfurling the faith

A. In order to make the spiritual progress we all long to make (Philippians 1:25), we need to unfurl the sails.

1. This will require some work on our part.

2. But it can be done, and the effort is worth it!

B. Let the wind of the Spirit fill the sails.

C. Let the Lord carry you across the sea of faith!

II

PAX ROMANA
Preparation for the First Coming

I. Why did Jesus not come earlier?

A. God was preparing a people (Galatians 3:24).

B. God was revealing himself progressively in a cumulative revelation (Hebrews 1:1).

C. Could people be saved under the Old Covenant?

1. Yes – analogy of debt guaranteed.

2. And yet no salvation apart from covenant (Romans 2:12).

D. Christ came at just the right time (1 Corinthians 10:11, 1 Timothy 2:6, etc).

ROMAN EMPIRE, 100 AD.–Study this map!

1. Born under Augustus, died under Tiberius

2. Caesar means emperor. (*Kaisar* in Greek, *Caesar* in Latin, *Czar* or *Tsar* in Russian, *Kaiser* in German...)

II. The Ancient Romans

A. Role of Augustus Caesar

B. Eclipse of Greeks in 2nd century BC

C. End of a century of civil war in late 1st century BC

Roman Emperors	
Augustus	27 BC-14 AD
Tiberius	14-37 AD
Caligula	37-41 AD
Claudius	41-54 AD
Nero	54-68 AD
Galba	68-69 AD
Otto	69 AD
Vitellius	69 AD
Vespasian	69-79 AD
Titus	79-81 AD
Domitian	81-96 AD

Ref: Suetonius, *Lives of the Twelve Caesars*

III. The Pax Romana

A. Communication

1. The Greek language
   a. Classical Greek
   b. Koine Greek
   c. Hellenistic Greek
   d. Modern Greek

B. Connections
   1. Roads
   2. Seaways
   3. Borders

C. Common culture

   1. Hellenization
      a. language
      b. literature
      c. arts
      d. gymnasium
      e. theater

   2. Outlook
      a. Anxiety and fatalism in ancient world
      b. Bankruptcy of traditional religions

D. Stability of Roman government

   1. A century of calm

   2. Imperial protection and privileges for Jews (includes Christians)

E. Conditions in the 21st century optimal

   1. Communication
      a. Dominant languages
      b. Role of English
      c. Internet

   2. Connections
      a. Air travel
      b. Postal system

   3. Outlook
      a. Diversity tolerated, openness to new things
      b. Authenticity, practicality, not just "truth"

   4. Relative stability

JESUS CHRIST
The Life and Death of Jesus

I. Life of Jesus

   A. Major events

   1. Birth – Matthew 1

   2. Family (mother, father, brothers, sisters)

   3. Childhood

   4. Baptism and temptation

   5. Public ministry

   6. Transfiguration (Old Testament connection)

   7. Passion week

II. Death and beyond

   A. Death

   B. Resurrection

   C. Instruction

   D. Ascension

   E. Return

III. Exaggerations and embellishments—the apocryphal gospels

A. These include such works as *The Lost Letter of St. Paul, The Gospel of Thomas, The Gospel of Philip, The Gospel of Peter, The Gospel of Truth,* and *The Acts of Pilate.*

B. Such works were authored generations—or centuries!—after the authentic first century gospels

C. One sample: *The Gospel of Thomas* (2nd century AD)

1. Tradition is strong that the apostle Thomas established the church in India sometime in the 40s. Although I started out skeptical about the various accounts, I have read enough now to be fairly convinced. I have even seen Thomas' tomb in south India. There seems little reason to doubt the veracity of the tradition.

2. The "gospel" attributed to him is another matter.

3. Thomas was considered by some Gnostics to be the twin brother of Jesus. "Judas Thomas the Twin" is the key phrase. The Egyptian Gnostics who created this "gospel" in fact identified Thomas with the Jude we know from the New Testament as one of Jesus' four brothers.

4. *The Gospel of Thomas* is increasingly popular these days, especially among people who want us to believe that the New Testament is not a complete or accurate record of what Jesus taught during his earthly ministry. Actually, this book, or collection of supposed sayings of Jesus, is not really a "gospel" at all, since the Passion narrative is totally absent. There is no emphasis either on self-sacrificing love, except possibly one saying about carrying one's cross.

5. Unlike the four canonical gospels, Thomas is only a sayings list.

6. The apostle Thomas had nothing to do with its creation.

7. The theology of the book, if there is a real theology, is Gnostic.
   a. Insight is more important than morality.
   b. Spirit is more real and significant than matter.
   c. Gnosticism is making a comeback today in the New Age Movement.
   d. This was a philosophy-religion that appealed to the ego, without requiring any real commitment.
   e. The Bible reader will recall that as early as Paul's own lifetime, Gnosticism was a growing threat to the nascent church. (See, for example, 1 Timothy, which is full of warnings about the Gnostic teachers.) Note: *Gnosis* is the Greek word for "knowledge"—as in 1 Timothy 6:20.

8. Manuscripts, complete or partial, have been found from the second and third centuries, so probably Thomas was written no later than about 100 or 150, and may possibly date even earlier.

9. The numbering of the following excerpts may vary slightly from edition to edition, but give the shortness of Thomas, you should have no trouble locating the original sayings if you decide to go further in your study.

The *Gospel of Thomas* (Excerpts) Prologue:

These are the secret sayings that the living Jesus spoke and Judas Thomas the Twin recorded.

Comment: Here is purported to be a "secret" source for a competing tradition about Jesus. Fragments of Thomas were discovered in the late 1800s, and by 1945 the Egyptian desert had begun to yield more or less complete copies. By reading these sayings, you enter an elite circle of persons who know what Jesus really said. Arcane sayings A number of sayings in Thomas seem to defy analysis. What did they mean? What was their original context? For example, consider the following two sayings. While explanations have been offered, no one really knows what the writer—whoever he was—meant to convey.

Saying 2: "*Jesus said, 'Let not him who seeks desist until he finds. When he finds he will be troubled; when he is troubled he will marvel, and he will reign over the universe.'*"

Saying 3: "*Jesus said, '...the kingdom is inside you and outside you'...*"

Saying 7: "*Jesus said, 'Happy is the lion whom the man eats, so that the lion becomes a man; but woe to the man whom the lion eats, so that the man becomes lion!'*" In short, because we do not understand what these sayings refer to, and because they are lacking the literary and historical contexts that would give us the necessary clues, they must remain shrouded in mystery. For all intents and purposes, they are arcane. Authentic sayings? Some of the sayings reflect the genuine gospel tradition. In fact, it is not possible to "prove" that none of these sayings is authentic—especially with a little imagination!

Saying 47: "*...a person cannot mount two horses or bend two bows, and a servant cannot serve two lords...*"

Saying 64: "*...Business people and merchants will not enter the realm of my Father.*" (This saying appears at the end of Thomas' version of the Parable of the Banquet. The beginning of the story is not especially problematic, despite its rather disturbing ending.)

Saying 98: "*...Give Caesar what is Caesar's, give God what is God's, and give me what is mine!*" Once again, there is no reason that some of Jesus' words unrecorded in the scriptures (John 21: 25) could not have found their way into various sayings sources. Yet who is to assay them? Who will assess whether they are authentic? Absurd sayings! The following three sayings reflect the Gnosticism of the early heretics, and the middle one appears to be pantheistic. (Pantheism is the doctrine that God is everything.) It is highly unlikely Jesus is the one behind any of them.

The Faith Unfurled

Saying 67: "Jesus said, 'He who knows the All and has no need but of himself has need everywhere.'"

Saying 77: "Jesus said, 'I am the light which shines upon all. I am the All; All has gone forth from me and All has come back to me. Cleave the wood, and there am I; raise the stone, and there you will find me.'"

Saying 113/114: "Simon Peter said to them, 'Let Mary leave us, because women are not worthy of life.' Jesus said, 'Behold, I shall guide her so as to make her male, so that she may become a living spirit like you men. For every woman who makes herself male will enter the kingdom of heaven."

Is the New Testament missing any books? Not at all. Nothing is "missing," because nothing was removed or lost. Quite simply, the early church did not recognize the authority of this "gospel"—nor has any part of Christianity subsequently. Next time your friends or workmates drop comments about the Gospel of Thomas, hopefully you will be well equipped to respond!

For further study in *The Gospel of Thomas,* translations from the original Coptic are easily obtainable. Try *The Secret Teachings of Jesus: Four Gnostic Gospels,* tr. Marvin W. Meyer (New York: Random House, 1984), or *Jesus and Christian Origins Outside the New Testament,* F. F. Bruce (London: Hodder & Stoughton, 1974).

IV. Early Christian symbols

A. Peacock

B. Anchor

C. Bread and fish

D. Cross

E. ☧ (Chi Rho)

F. AΩ (Alpha Omega)

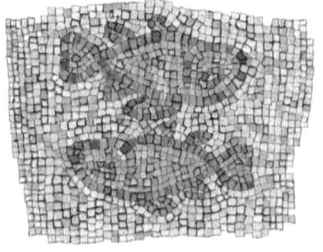

G. Lily

H. Phoenix

I. Shepherd

J. Wheat

K. INRI

L. IXθYC (Ichthus)

V. Conclusion

A. We do not know what he looked like – yet we recognize his image in all who are born of God.

B. He left us nothing in writing – and yet he is the Word of God, and through his Spirit the New Testament was inspired and given to us as a precious gift.

C. He told us he's coming back, but we do not know when. We must strive to live in expectation and preparation. As the Lord asked, "When the Son of Man returns, will he find faith on the earth?" (Luke 18:8b)

IV
THE SYNOPTIC GOSPELS
Matthew, Mark, and Luke

I. General

A. Authors

1. Matthew—apostle, writing in third person

2. Luke—associate of Paul, only Gentile author in Bible, writing in first person

3. Mark—associate of Peter, writing in third person

   "Mark, having become the interpreter of Peter, wrote down accurately whatever he remembered. It was not, however, in exact order that he related the sayings or deeds of Christ. For he neither heard the Lord nor accompanied Him. But afterwards, as I said, he accompanied Peter, who accommodated his instructions to the necessities [of his hearers], but with no intention of giving a regular narrative of the Lord's sayings... He took special care not to omit anything he had heard, and not to put anything fictitious into the statements."
   —Papias, 125 AD

B. Length: Luke—Matthew—Mark

C. Language: Greek, except (possibly) for Matthew

   Gk: Ἐν ἀρχῇ ἦν ὁ λόγος, καὶ ὁ λόγος ἦν πρὸς τὸν θεόν, καὶ θεὸς ἦν ὁ λόγος.

   Heb: אַשְׁרֵי־הָאִישׁ אֲשֶׁר לֹא הָלַךְ בַּעֲצַת רְשָׁעִים

   Lat (secondary language): In principio erat Verbum et Verbum erat apud Deum...

D. Date
  1. Letters (40s+) preceded gospels (60s+)
  2. Mark precedes other synoptic gospels
  3. Key event is destruction of Jerusalem & Temple, 70 AD

E. Matthew, Mark, and Luke
  1. Common view. The meaning of "synoptic"
  2. Common thread: Caesarea Philippi → Jerusalem
  3. Common material (parables, mini-apocalypse, passion account, great commission)
  4. Literary relationship

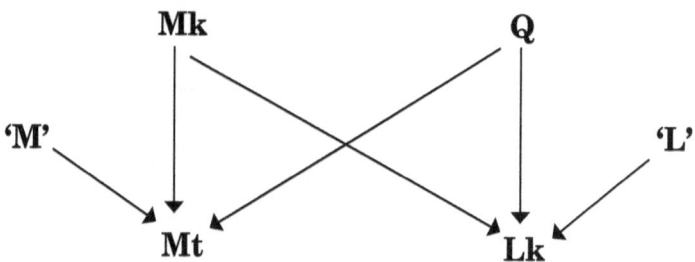

F. Themes
  1. Matthew
     a. For Jews
        (1) Five teaching blocks (5:1-7:29, 10:11-42, 13:1-52, 18:1-35, [23:1] 24:1-25:46). Matthew mirrors the Torah (Pentateuch)
        (2) Old Testament fulfillment formulae used 11x.
        (3) Gentile mission—fulfillment of Genesis 12:3 (promise to Abram)

2. Mark
   a. For practical minded Romans
      (1) "Immediately"; swift action!
      (2) Jesus is kingly Messiah and the suffering servant of Isaiah
      (3) His identity is to be concealed (for a while)
      (4) Israel to undergo a new exodus (major motif of Isaiah)
      (5) Matthew and Luke apparently use Mark as a primary source.

3. Luke
   a. Gentiles
   b. For all people
      (1) Luke (part 1)—salvation for all strata of society (vertical)
      (2) Acts (part 2)—salvation of all geographical regions of society (horizontal)
   b. Marginalized persons
   c. The Spirit
   d. Prayer
   e. Isaiah and nation of Israel

V

THE FOURTH GOSPEL
The Gospel of John

I. General

　A.　Author

　B.　Date

　C.　Textual basis and p^{52}

　D.　The Johannine corpus

II. How John is Different to the Synoptics

　A.　Story told from perspective of time after resurrection and Spirit.

　B.　Spans several years, not one.

　C.　May be structured around seven "signs" (2:11, 4:54, [5:9], 6:14, 9:16, 11:47, [21:1-14], although other "signs" are referred to in John as well (for instance, 2:23, 3:2, 6:2, and 20:30).

　D.　Ministry set primarily in Jerusalem, not Galilee

　E.　Narrative genre

III. Special emphases in John

A. "I am" statements

B. Physical v. spiritual confusion. Words have double meanings.

C. Similarities to 1 John. Big emphasis on Jesus' humanity.

D. Jesus is incarnate Word. Philosophical prologue.

IV. Through John

A. Thoughts from chapter 1

B. Thoughts from chapter 2

C. Thoughts from chapters 20-21

V. CONCLUSION

A. Cosmic dimension!

B. "If the Synoptic Gospels care about Jesus' place in the history of Israel and beyond, John cares about Jesus' place in the whole scheme of things—from creation to redemption and beyond (final resurrection). That the Messiah is none other than the eternal Son of God is the ultimate good news of the Christian story."
—Gordon Fee, *How to Read the Bible Book by Book,* p. 313.

C. 4-d view!

VI

CONTRADICTIONS?
Handling Bible Difficulties

I. Introduction

  A. Four gospels afford four distinct angles or perspectives on the life of Jesus. Better than one!

  B. Necessary in order for us to appreciate who Jesus Christ really is.

  C. And yet the details do not always seem to match up.

  D. This leads to the broader question of how to approach "contradictions" in the Bible.

II. General strategies

  A. Look closer. Surface contradictions usually disappear with closer scrutiny

  B. Take language into account. Original Semitic language(s) → Greek → modern language

  C. Realize that chronology is less important than theology.

  D. Harmonize

  E. Appreciate the flexibility of the Holy Spirit.

   1. Selection

   2. Arrangement

3. Adaptation

4. Identify distinctive emphases; don't blend everything together. Ask, "What is the Spirit trying to show here? Why is this passage included in the Bible?"

III. Addressing questions (adapted from *Compelling Evidence for God and the Bible,* Appendix C, 2010 edition)

A. Introduction

1. "Name one!"
That's what I say whenever someone comes out with the familiar "Everyone knows the Bible is full of contradictions." Usually the person, caught completely off guard, cannot think of even one of the "many" contradictions he believes exist in the Bible. Other times the doubt may be genuine, and usually a satisfying answer can be found. Certainly I'm not implying that every part of the Bible is easy to understand, but in most cases, the "contradiction" turns out to be a misunderstanding that clears up after a second reading or a little further study.

2. The test of consistency
God's word is consistent on two levels. It is without *external* inconsistencies (where known facts of science, logic, history, archaeology, geography, etc. are contradicted) and *internal* inconsistencies (where one part of the message contradicts another part). However, some people claim to see inconsistencies where there are none and they call them "contradictions." Let's have a look at some kinds of *false* contradictions.

B. False contradictions

1. Differences in Translation Among Versions
No modern translation of the Hebrew and Greek text is perfect, though some versions are more accurate than others. For example, the word translated

"disciples" (Acts 11:26) in the more accurate translations (like the NIV, RSV, KJV and NAS) is incorrectly rendered "believers" in the paraphrased *Living Bible*. There is, of course, no contradiction in the original text.

2. Lack of Scientific Precision

The Bible was never intended to be a science textbook. It often speaks of "sunrise" and "sunset," although through astronomy we know that technically it is the earth that moves, not the sun. Yet we ourselves continue to speak of "sunrise"—that does not mean that we are ignorant or "wrong." Can you imagine Genesis 1 ("In the beginning God created...") if it were rewritten "scientifically": "At the alpha point of space-time the Supreme Being so ordered the Cosmos that conditions favorable for the synthesis of deoxyribonucleic acid came to exist within a mere eleven billion years"? Ancient readers would have been baffled, as most of us modern readers are!

Also, lack of scientific precision is characteristic of the Bible's poetry—which is exactly where we take the greatest liberties in modern language. (Poetry typically uses words and concepts to evoke images and emotions.)

Consider Psalm 18:8-10:

Smoke rose from his nostrils;
　　consuming fire came from his mouth,
burning coals blazed out of it.
　　He parted the heavens and came down;
dark clouds were under his feet.
　　He mounted the cherubim and flew;
he soared on the wings of the wind.

Physically, the heavens cannot be parted, the wind has no wings, and smoke and fire would destroy anyone's nostrils! This colorful language is not a true instance of contradiction; it is *poetry*. Lack of scientific precision is not a true contradiction. On the other hand, there are a number of places in which the Bible demonstrates remarkable scientific insight.

3. Approximations

   We understand that the Bible often uses round numbers and other approximations—especially where large quantities are involved. (For example, Matthew 14:21, the feeding of the 5,000.) Similarly, Biblical writers did not feel a burden to report the exact words when they recorded a conversation. Speeches, for example, are condensed. In fact, everything Jesus said that is recorded in the Bible can be read through aloud in just a couple of hours! Surely he spoke more than two hours in his three-year ministry, but how fortunate it is that the Bible didn't record everything—the Gospels alone would be tens of thousands of pages long. Abbreviations and approximations must not be seen as contradictions.

4. Differences with Other Ancient Sources

   a. Josephus, a Jewish politician and writer living from 33 to 100 AD, records the uprising of Judas the Galilean as well as the census under Quirinius, but places them at a different point chronologically from where the Bible locates them (Josephus, *Antiquities 20.5.2.* versus Acts 5:37, Luke 2:2). But why should the benefit of the doubt be extended to Josephus? Why not to the Biblical text? Liberal scholars and others eager to disprove the Bible not surprisingly favor Josephus and other extra-Biblical writers whenever there is a contradiction with the Scriptures. This bias is neither called for nor acceptable from a scholarly perspective!

   b. *Thousands* of discoveries have been made confirming the record of the Bible—and yet there are still thousands of sites waiting to be explored. Since the Bible has not been proven wrong up to this point, if there's a dispute, it would seem wisest not to draw any hasty conclusions concerning contradictions.[2]

5. Minor Chronological Differences
   Ancient writers did not have the same concern for strict time sequence that we have. (Not that a man's

death would be recorded as happening before his birth, of course!) For example, the temptations of Jesus are recorded in Matthew 4 in the order 1-2-3. Luke 4, however, lists them in the order 1-3-2. This is hardly a contradiction, for the details of the two temptation accounts are identical. On the whole, Bible writers were at least as careful about chronology as any other ancient writers. (See Luke 2:1-2, 3:1-2.)

6. Spelling Variations in Different Ancient Manuscripts

Psalm 100:3 reads, "It is he who made us, and we are his." Earlier versions read, "It is he who made us, and not we ourselves." The solution: In the older translation the Hebrew word *lo* (his) was mistaken for the word *lo'* (not), because of a common spelling variant. Even in English, standardized spelling is a fairly recent development, having happened only in the last couple of centuries. For example, on opposite sides of the Atlantic we find hundreds of differences: "honour" instead of "honour," "tyre" instead of "tire," etc. No, we must not fault the various Biblical writers for grammatical, syntactical, phonological, morphological or orthographical variations! (These are very long words but not contradictions.)

7. Minor Variations from One Manuscript to Another

Jesus found the demon-possessed man (Mark 5:1) in the region of the Gerasenes—or was it Gadarenes? Or the Gergesenes? Scholars are not sure which reading is the original one. But does it really matter? No surviving manuscript is an exact copy of the original NT and OT writings, although many ancient manuscripts are nearly exact copies. The alternative readings listed in the footnotes of your Bible are not "contradictions"—they are simply instances in which translators were unsure of the correct reading. The principle is this: Inspiration applies to the original text, not to copies. However, most differences are so minor that it would be tiresome to list them. None of the above are true contradictions, and if we understand this, we will not run into difficulty very often.

C. Solutions to Apparent Contradictions

Following are a number of apparent contradictions. As we study each one, there will be a valuable lesson to keep in mind when you think you may have found a contradiction in the Bible.

1. Two Sides of a Coin

    Romans 3:28 and James 2:24: In Romans Paul says that we are made right with God "by faith apart from observing the law," while James says, "you see that a person is justified by what he does and not by faith alone." Who is right, Paul or James? This "contradiction" was so disturbing to Martin Luther that the sixteenth century Protestant reformer decided to insert the word "alone" after faith in his personal translation of Romans 3:28. (At one point he even stated that James should be thrown out of the Bible!) But the solution is not hard to understand: True faith always proves itself in deeds, or as James says, faith without deeds is dead (James 2:26). Faith without deeds is not true faith. Neither Paul nor James is confused—what both of them wrote is inspired by God, and through their letters, God tells us the truth about a right relationship with him. In this supposed contradiction we see that the two views are really two sides of the same coin and fit together nicely. Often a seeming contradiction resolves itself when we just take the time to be reasonable and think it through.

2. Missing Information

    Matthew 27:45 and John 19:14: In Matthew's account of the crucifixion, by the "sixth hour" Jesus had been on the cross for some time, whereas in the gospel of John he is still before Pilate on the Stone Pavement. Was Matthew confused, or was John the confused one? And how could their stories differ so much if they were both in Jerusalem when their Master was executed? This does not seem to be the kind of "minor" chronological difference we have discussed above. Neither was confused because they were following different time-keeping systems! Matthew, whose gospel is the most Jewish of the four gospels, was following the Jewish system of time keeping. The sixth hour is actually midday, and Jesus died at the ninth hour or, 3:00 PM. John, on the other hand, who was writing for a non-Jewish audience, was following the Roman method, which is like our own. In John the sixth hour was 6:00 AM. After Pontius Pilate decided to have Jesus executed, the soldiers abused him for a while (Matthew 27:27)—there was still plenty of time before the crucifixion. This particular contradiction would have been quite difficult to resolve without the missing information, which most Bibles would not supply. Again, if you have found a problem, it is probably best not to call it a "contradiction" until you have tried hard to reach a solution.

3. Beware of Assumptions

   Deuteronomy 34: Here we read of the death of Moses—which is remarkable, since Moses is supposed to have written Deuteronomy! This one really seems overwhelming! After all, there are only so many things a dead man can do. How did he do it? He didn't, any more than Jesus took notes on his own crucifixion. We must be aware (or beware) of our presuppositions. It is widely believed that Moses is the author of all of Deuteronomy. If he was not, the contradiction vanishes. My own view is that while Moses was primarily responsible for Deuteronomy, edited after his death, he clearly did not write his own obituary. Often people *assume* the Bible says something it never says. Contrary to popular belief, the Bible never states when the earth was created. The date "4004 BC" was a very uninspired guess by an otherwise intelligent archbishop a few centuries ago, but many have actually taught this as the date of creation! Let's consider some other assumptions. The Bible never says there were *three* wise men bearing gifts for the infant Jesus. All it mentions is that there were three different kinds of gifts (Matthew 2:11). Here's a final example: Do you envision angels as having wings? Where does the Bible say that? It doesn't—probably we think of angels as having wings because of the Renaissance paintings.

4. A Little Imagination

   Matthew 27:5 and Acts 1:18: About the death of Judas—in Matthew's account he hanged himself, while Luke (who wrote Acts) said that he spilt his intestines in a field. Who's right? (By this time you are cautious about choosing sides!) Do we really think that Luke, the careful historian (see Luke 1:1-4) would contradict Matthew, one of Jesus' original apostles? It appears that someone (other than Judas) threw Judas' body into the field, so that it "burst open and all his intestines spilled out" (Acts 1:18). Perhaps Judas had been dead for some time, perhaps not. Or perhaps Judas fell when he was cut down from the tree from which he hanged himself—perhaps not. At any rate, the precise solution is irrelevant; there is no necessary contradiction, and it doesn't take a lot of imagination to think of a solution.

5. Look Before You Leap!

   Matthew 8:5 and Luke 7:3: In Matthew's account of the healing of the centurion's servant, the centurion appears to go personally to ask Jesus to heal his servant, whereas in Luke we read that he sent some elders of the Jews to put the question to Jesus. Which is right? Yes, they're both right. The centurion authorized the elders to go on his behalf; it was not necessary that he be there himself. In the same way, someone might say, "You brought my car to the station last week, didn't you?" Would I be a deceiver if I said, "That's right," even though I actually had my wife bring in the car? Isn't this an acceptable way of putting things? Yes. It is possible to be overly strict in our interpretations, and we must be careful that we have the full picture before jumping to conclusions—or convulsions. Often a parallel passage in another part of the Bible helps to resolve the apparent contradiction. The old adage seems appropriate: Look before you leap!

6. Summary

   The Bible is never at odds with science, history or logic. Science and the Bible are good friends; they work hand in glove to help us understand our world and ourselves.

Nor is any discovery of historians or archaeologists going to cause the walls of Christian faith to come tumbling down! People have tried to bring the walls down for 2,000 years, but they stand as solid as ever. And regarding logic: the more we think about the truth, the more likely we are to end up seeing things God's way—because the Christian faith is both true and reasonable. The Bible has some confusing passages, but no problem disproves any of the fundamental teachings of the Bible. We should never let the parts we can't yet understand keep us from obeying the parts we can understand!

IV. Conclusion (review)

A. Look closer. Surface contradictions disappear with closer scrutiny.

B. Take language into account. Original Semitic language(s) → Greek → modern language

C. Realize that chronology is less important than theology

D. Harmonize

E. Appreciate the flexibility of the Holy Spirit.

   1. Selection

   2. Arrangement

   3. Adaptation

   4. Identify distinct emphases.

F. Remember this: Exact correspondence = forgery!

VII

THE FIRST GENERATION
The Book of Acts and How to Read it

I. The function and reliability of Acts

   A. Introductory matters

      1. The "church history" book of the New Testament

      2. Time perspectives
        a. Gospels → Acts ← Letters
        b. Time span: about 30 years, from 30-60 AD.
          (1) Does not mesh with chronology of Pastoral Epistles.
          (2) This suggests Paul was released after Acts 28.

      3. Selectivity. Ask, "What the Holy Spirit is trying to convey?"

      4. Theophilus (Luke 1:3, Acts 1:1). Note: Theophilus means "God-lover."
        a. Luke's literary patron?
        b. Fictional character—literary device?
        c. Non-Christian Luke wants to influence?
        d. A Roman whom Luke wants to influence?

      5. Acts is "volume II" of Luke
        a. Volume III planned but interrupted
        b. Luke-Acts meant to be 2 volumes only – a brief for trial in Rome
        c. Luke-Acts 2 volumes only because Paul killed; all knew outcome
        d. Luke-Acts does not cover Paul's evangelism after release from prison

The Faith Unfurled

      6. Other names for this book
         a. Acts of Peter and Paul
         b. Acts of the Holy Spirit
         b. "Acts" a literary genre: (apocryphal *Acts of Paul, Acts of Pilate, Peter, Paul and Thecla,* etc)

  B. Rooted in reality

      1. Geography
         a. Luke mentions 95 cities, islands, countries, etc in Luke-Acts— no errors
         b. Can visit many of these places: Israel, Turkey, Malta
         c. Archaeological and literary verification (Jerusalem has abundant artifacts; Corinth has the Erastus pavement and synagogue inscription; Athens has the Areopagus; Caesarea has the Pilate inscription; many other things—Miletus agora, such technical terms as "Asiarch," Temple of Artemis, etc)

      2. Chronological checks
         a. 30-60 AD—span of 30 years
         b. Gallio inscription (Corinth)
         c. Years of reign of Felix, Festus, Agrippa, Herod Agrippa
         d. Expulsion of Jews from Rome (49 AD)

  C. Lots of surprises

      1. The elegance of the writing style

      2. 1000s of baptisms in one day (*mikvaoth*).

      3. Ananias and Sapphira drop dead! ("God of the O.T.")

      4. 7 sons of Sceva!

      5. And many more!

II. How to Read Acts

  A. Compare and contrast with Luke.

1. *Luke in reverse:* From Galilee to Jerusalem; A—from Jerusalem to Gentile territory

2. *Complementary to Luke:* Gospel for every social stratum (vertically); A—gospel for every region (horizontally)

B. Respect the structure

1. Jerusalem to Rome
   (|| Synoptics: Caesarea → Jerusalem)

2. Structure: phases of evangelism. 1:8 is the key verse. Six "panels"
   a. Jerusalem (1:1-6:7)
   b. Judea and Samaria (6:8-9:31)
   c. Gentiles and conversion of Paul (9:32-12:24)
   d. Asia (12:25-16:5)
   e. Europe (16:6-19:20)
   f. To Rome, capital of Gentile world (19:21-28:31)

3. Outpouring (depending on ascension)—4 remarkable manifestations, 4 different circumstances. (See *The Spirit* for a fuller explanation.)
   a. Jerusalem (chapter 2)
   b. Samaria (chapter 8)
   c. Caesarea (chapter 10)
   d. Ephesus (chapter 19)

4. Division between ministry of Peter and ministry of Paul
   a. Peter 1-12, Paul 13-28.
   b. In life of Paul, there are 4 (missionary) journeys
      family devotional ide

5. Understand the role of the speeches, which appear at crucial points and show how the gospel is presented and defended in a variety of differing settings. (See *A Quick Overview of the Bible*).

6. Be aware of the major themes
   a. Spirit
   b. Kingdom
   c. Repentance
   d. Resurrection
   e. Possessions and wealth
   f. The place of women
   g. The poor and marginalized of society

7. Beware patternism
   a. Acts 2:42!
   b. Acts 20:7ff!

III. Conclusion

A. Read Acts with the intention to obey!

B. Aim to be injected with the spirit of faith that animated the early church. Take the book personally.

VIII
PAUL I
The Life and Death of Paul

I. Why three chapters on Paul?

A. Jesus and Paul are beyond question the two personages of the New Testament about whom we know most.

B. Paul wrote 13 of the 27 New Testament documents. 87 chapters (compared to 89 chapters in the gospels).

C. He thought, taught, and wrote at the deepest level, theologically speaking, of any of the 9 or so New Testament writers.

D. We are able to coordinate his missionary activities (Acts) with his writing and follow-up ministry (the letters).

II. The Life of Paul

A. Pharisee (Acts 22:3, 23:6, 26:5, 2 Corinthians 11:22, Galatians 1:14, Philippians 3:5)

 1. The four major sects of Judaism in the 1st century
    a. Pharisees
    b. Sadducees
    c. Zealots+
    d. Essenes

 2. Distinctive beliefs of Pharisees
    a. Resurrection
    b. Scripture
    c. Oral law

B. Paul and his contemporaries

   1. Motivation (Galatians 1:13-14)

   2. Conscience (Acts 23:1, 24:16)

   3. Understand him better by reading from the bibliography on Judaism.

> Short bibliography shedding light on Judaism:
> - Alfred Edersheim, *Bible History: Old Testament* (Peabody, Mass.: Hendrickson, 1995); *Sketches of Jewish Social Life* (Peabody, Mass.: Hendrickson, 1994); *The Temple: Its Ministry and Services* (Peabody, Mass.: Hendrickson, 1994).
> - Walter Kaiser, *A History of Israel* (Nashville: Broadman & Holman, 1998)
> - Jacob Neusner, *Between Time and Eternity: The Essentials of Judaism* (Belmont, Cal.: Wadsworth, 1975); *Invitation to the Talmud: A Teaching Book* (San Francisco: Harper, 1984); *The Mishnah: A New Translation* (New Haven: Yale University Press, 1988)
> - Emil Schürer, *The History of the Jewish People in the Age of Jesus Christ (175 BC-AD 135)*, (Edinburgh: T.&T. Clark, 1973)
> - Hershel Shanks, *Jerusalem: An Archaeological Biography* (New York: Random House, 1995); (Ed.) *Understanding the Dead Sea Scrolls: A Reader from the Biblical Archaeological Review* (New York: Random House, 1992)
> - William Whiston, Tr., *Josephus' Complete Works* (Grand Rapids: Kregel, 1973)
> - Michael Wise, Martin Abegg, Jr. & Edward Cook, *The Dead Sea Scrolls: A New Translation* (San Francisco: Harper, 1996)

C. Family

   1. Unclear whether he was married

2. Many relatives became Christians—Andronicus and Junias (Romans 16:7); Herodion (Romans 16:11; Lucius, Jason, Sosipater (Romans 16:21), sister and nephew? (Acts 23:16)

D. Various personal details

  1. Citizen (Acts 16:37, 22:25-28)

  2. Tarsus (Acts 9:11, 21:39, 22:3)

  3. Tribe of Benjamin (Romans 11:1, Philippians 3:5)

  4. Trained under Gamaliel (Acts 22:3, 26:4)

  5. Presence and role at execution of Stephen (Acts 7:58, 8:1, 8:3; 9:1; 22:4)

  6. Damascus Road experience (Acts 9, 22, 26)

  7. Tentmaker (Acts 18:3)

  8. Apostle with a capital 'A'
     a. Eyewitness of resurrection (Acts 1:22, 1 Corinthians 9:1)
     b. Hand-picked by Jesus to receive revelation (e.g. Galatians 1:12; many vv. in Acts; see John 14:26, 16:13)

  9. Progressive humility in self-assessment
     a. 1 Corinthians 15:9
     b. Ephesians 3:8
     c. 1 Timothy 1:15

  10. Unimpressive in appearance? (2 Corinthians 10:10)

The Faith Unfurled

E. Chronology

  1. Baptized around 34 AD

  2. If Paul is an "old man" (Philemon 9) ca. 61 AD, presumably 60, then he was born ca. 1 AD. (Note: "Young man" [Acts 7:58] would easily apply to a man not yet 40.) Executed by 68 AD. For more on the chronology of Paul's life, see chapter 18.

III. The death of Paul

A. What church tradition says—beheaded at Aquae Salviae along the Appian Way, just outside Rome. (See F. F. Bruce, *Paul: Apostle of the Heart Set Free* (Grand Rapids: Eerdmans, 1977), 450-451.)

B. What the Bible says—2 Timothy 4 (his last letter)

IX
PAUL II
Letters to Churches and Paul's Philosophy of Missions

I. How the letters to churches are arranged

A. Letters of Paul

   1. Nine letters to churches, longest to shortest

   2. Four letters to individuals, longest to shortest

B. Other letters

   1. Hebrews (Pauline connection)

   2. Seven letters of James, Peter, John, and Jude

   3. Seven letters of Revelation 2-3

II General advice on how to read epistles

A. Remember that they are written to converted insiders.

   1. Understand that the addressees already understood the *gospel*, even though the *gospels* hadn't yet been written.

   2. Reminiscences and records of the words and deeds of Jesus were undoubtedly current and frequently referred to.

B. Notice the emphases (root and fruit, Acts 2)...

The Faith Unfurled

C. Remember that they were read aloud and publicly more than read silently and privately.

D. Remember that you may be hearing one side of a conversation. 1 Corinthians as an example.

E. Questions of context and culture are inescapable. E.g., 2 Timothy 4:2, 13.

F. Where possible, correlate with events in Acts. E.g., Paul visited Corinth (Acts 18) and then moved on to Ephesus (Acts 19), from which he wrote 1 Corinthians (1 Corinthians 16:7).

G. For those in Christ 5-10 years and who are diligent students of the New Testament, "must" reading is Fee & Stuart, *How to Read the Bible For All Its Worth* (see bibliography).

III. Specific advice on how to read Paul's letters to churches (all dates provisional)

• Galatians (48 AD)—His first surviving letter. Realize that Paul's anger comes from the very serious threat to the gospel. People's salvation is at stake.

• 1-2 Thessalonians (50 AD)—After three Sabbath days' work in Thessalonica, Paul pens two letters to strengthen believers.

• 1 Corinthians (55 AD)—Paul responds to a concerning report *and* a letter from the Corinthians. 2 Corinthians (56 AD)—Paul responds to challenges to this authority, and makes a key point about leadership and suffering.

• Romans (56 AD)—The strategic purpose of Romans: unity among Jews and Gentiles.

• Ephesians (60 AD)—Realize that among the churches in Asia, some preachers are pressuring Gentile Christians to conform to Judaism. There is also anxiety about fate/the powers/astrology.

- Philippians (60 AD)—Realize that Philippi is a Roman colony, where the Emperor Cult and suppression of Christianity challenge the believers' joy.

- Colossians (60 AD)—Keep in mind that Paul is dealing with false teaching. Christ is the answer, not external rule-keeping or a return to Judaism, Paul insists. Further, the short letter of Philemon may have been delivered along with Colossians to the church. (Compare the two letters.)

IV. A philosophy of missions

- Fellow workers (e.g. Acts 20:4)

- Concentrate on the cities (pattern of Acts)

- Jews first, then Gentiles (Romans 1:16)

- Appoint local leadership

- Fresh territory if possible (Romans 15:19-24)

- It takes money (1 Corinthians 9:12; 2

PAUL III
Letters to individuals, pastoral epistles, church governance

I. Pastoral Epistles and church governance

A. Three letters (1-2 Timothy and Titus) are called "pastoral" epistles. Note: "Pastor" is the Latin word for shepherd. Paul is helping his assistants exercise pastoral care over the congregations they serve.

B. They are all written in the mid- to late-60s, a full generation after Pentecost. Thus they afford a glimpse of issues facing the church in the second generation.

C. Into a new generation of Christianity

  1. First generation (30-60)—strong foundation
     a. Apostolic presence; effect of eyewitnesses; foundation laid by New Testament apostles, and prophets (Ephesians 2:20).
     b. Gentile mission during latter part of this generation (Acts 13 forward).
     c. God gradually weans the (Jewish) church away from its prejudices.

  2. Second generation (60-90)—drifting?
     a. Waning apostolic presence and waxing pseudoprophetic and pseudomessianic presence (2 Peter 2:1-3 etc).
     b. Church family dysfunction and general cooling off (Matthew 24:12)
     c. Regrouping in a time of transition.

> **Recommending Reading**
>
> W. M. Ramsay, *The Letters to the Seven Churches* (Peabody, Mass.: Hendrickson, 1994);
> J. B. Lightfoot, tr., *The Apostolic Fathers, Second Edition* (London: Apollos, 1989);
> William Barclay, *The Letters to Timothy, Titus, and Philemon* (Daily Study Bible Series)
> Alexander Strauch, *Biblical Eldership: An Urgent Call to Restore Biblical Church Leadership* (Littleton, Colorado: Lewis & Roth, 1995)

3. Into the third generation (90-120)
   a. 1 Clement (96 AD)—rebellion of younger leaders at Corinth against the eldership (power struggle).
   b. Gradual emergence of clergy.
   c. Increasing doctrinal drift.
      (1) By the late 100s, most church leaders accept the Old Testament Apocrypha as scripture.
      (2) The clergy class was slowly emerging.
      (3) Celibacy was receiving greater and greater honor. Many martyrs longed for death, with a morbid desire to be immolated or dismembered.

II. Letters to individuals

A. 1-2 Timothy

  1. Written after Paul's release from Roman imprisonment, or house arrest (Acts 28). 1 Timothy was written first! Titus came between it and 2 Timothy, Paul's final epistle.

  2. Addressed primarily to Timothy, but *you plural* in 1 Timothy 6:21 and 2 Timothy 4:22 implies it would have been shared with the congregation in Ephesus (1:3) as well.

B. About Timothy

  1. The man: 2 Timothy 1:5—Lois and Eunice—Jewish

Christians; unnamed father—pagan (Greek).
1 Timothy 5:23—Illnesses. Occasional encouragements to others to respect him suggest he wasn't as manly or impressive as some other leaders. And yet see Hebrews 13:23—Timothy, like Paul, is imprisoned for his faithfulness.

2. Timothy and Paul: Acts 16:1ff.—Paul recruits Timothy, circumcises him, and trains him. Acts 16 14—with Silas, Timothy gains leadership experience in Berea and many other places. Acts 20:4—there were other "Timothys," but 1 Corinthians 4 and Philippians 2 indicate Paul thought this man was unique. Timothy co-authored with Paul 2 Corinthians, Philippians, Colossians, 1-2 Thessalonians, and Philemon. Collaboration, from events of Acts 16 to those of 2 Timothy, spanned nearly 20 years of partnership.

3. Timothy's city (Ephesus)
    a. Located in western Turkey. A coastal city, now lying several miles inland. Fourth city of Empire, after Rome, Alexandria, Antioch. Population 200k.
    b. Here the cult of the Mother Goddess was very strong. Artemis (Diana) worshiped (Acts 19). Her servants were "honeybees." Temple in 16 out of 24 lists is one of "the seven wonders of the ancient world."(Which also included the Great Pyramid of Egypt, the Hanging Gardens of Babylon, the Statue of Zeus at Olympia, the Mausoleum of Halicarnassus, the Lighthouse of Alexandria, and the Colossus of Rhodes.) Pure marble, enormous building (425' x 225')—twice as long as Parthenon!
    c. The Ephesian Christian community:
        (1) Acts 19—the church is established (52 AD)
        (2) 1 Timothy—the church leader is counseled (65 AD) how best to strengthen the congregation.
            i. Enemies of the gospel have arisen from within the Ephesian eldership.
            ii. Fulfilled Paul's prediction in Acts 20:28-31.
            iii. They were taking advantage of younger widows (2 Timothy 3:6-7).

iv Paul mentions of couple of them by name, whom he had earlier disfellowshipped 1 Timothy 1:20).
(3) Revelation 2—the church is warned (69 or 96 AD)
(4) Ignatius' letter—the church has bounced back (107 AD).

Selections from Ignatius' letter to the Ephesians, c. 107 AD:

"Ignatius, who is also called God-bearer [Theophorus], to the church at Ephesus in Asia... I welcome in God your well-beloved name which you possess by reason of your righteous nature, which is characterized by faith in and love of Christ Jesus our Savior. Being as you are imitators of God, once you took on new life through the blood of God you completed perfectly the task so natural to you... Let no one deceive you, just as you are not now deceived, seeing that you belong entirely to God... You are all fellow pilgrims... Pray continually for the rest of mankind as well, that they may find God, for there is in them hope for repentance. Therefore allow them to be instructed by you—at least by your deeds... Therefore make every effort to come together more frequently to give thanks and glory to God. For when you meet together frequently, the powers of Satan are overthrown and his destructiveness is nullified by the unanimity of your faith... Continue to gather together, each and every one of you, collectively and individually by name, in grace, in one faith and one Jesus Christ, who physically was a descendant of David, who is Son of man and Son of God, in order that you may obey the overseer and the eldership with an undisturbed mind, breaking one bread, which is the medicine of immortality, the antidote we take in order not to die but to live forever in Jesus Christ... Remember me, as Jesus Christ does you. Pray for the church in Syria, from where I am being led to Rome in chains, as I—the very least of the faithful here—have been judged worthy of serving the glory of God. Farewell in God the Father and in Jesus Christ, our common hope."

4. Similar cosmopolitan societies and cosmopolitan issues as in the 21st century!

B. Titus

1. Written in mid-60s to Titus, whose charge is to appoint elders in every city

2. About Titus
   a. Unlike Timothy, had been raised as a Gentile (Galatians 2:3). Mentioned 14x in the New Testament, he had many great qualities (2 Corinthians 7:13-14, 8:6, 8:16-17, 12:18).
   b. Titus and Paul: They had a close bond and working relationship (2 Corinthians 2:13, 7:6, 8:23; Galatians 2:1, 2:3; 2 Timothy 4:10; Titus 1:4).

3. Paul wrote "Pastoral Epistles" so that, in his absence, error might be refuted and the needs of the churches met. Elderships to be established. (Ephesus had had elders for some 12 years by the time 1 Timothy was penned.)

4. Titus' territory (Crete)
   a. A sizeable island in the eastern Mediterranean. "Crete of the hundred cities" (Homer, 900 BC).
   b. Its evangelization is not mentioned in Acts (despite Acts 27:7, 12, 13, 21), though we find there are churches there by the time of Titus 1:5.
   c. Sinful tendencies deep in (Cretan) society, says Epimenides of Knossos (6th BC) in Titus 1:12.
      i. Lying and cheating part of stereotypical Cretan. *"Kretidzein."*
      ii. Epimenides the Cretan was invited to Athens in 596 BC, and was considered one of the seven wise men of ancient Greece.

C. Philemon

   1. Written along with Colossians (see Colossians 4:16) for an intriguing possibility.

2. A fascinating triple-study
   a. A Christian approach to a significant and sensitive social issue
   b. The institution of slavery
   c. Non-authoritarian leadership and persuasion

3. Onesimus, according to tradition, eventually became the overseer of the church in Ephesus.

III. Conclusion

A. Paul wrote to groups of Christians. He also wrote to individuals—but even then his letters were intended to be read by the larger Christian community. Under the influence and guidance of the Holy Spirit, he was truly writing for posterity.

B. Further study: One of the very best books on the apostle Paul is Ben Witherington III, *The Paul Quest*. For further titles, see bibliography in chapter 22.

HEBREWS
The Two Covenants, functions of Hebrews, Jewish Christianity and the end of a generation

I. The two covenants

A. Both covenants are covenants of grace. No one was saved by law-keeping under the old covenant! There is a tremendous emphasis on grace in the OT.

B. Although we aren't justified by law, we still aim to fulfill "the law of Christ" (Galatians 6:2).

C. Hebrews compares and contrasts the two covenants.

D. Key chapter: Hebrews 8

   1. Under the Old Testament, people already in the covenant had to be taught to know the Lord.

   2. Today, people "know the Lord" from the point they enter the covenant.

E. For more information, please see the study *Old Covenant, New Covenant* in *Till the Nets Are Full,* pg. 162 (IP: 2018).

II. The function of Hebrews

A. Introduction

   1. Author?
      a. Paul
      b. Luke

       c. Clement
       d. Barnabas
       e. Apollos
       f. Priscilla
       g. Philip
       h. Peter
       j. Silas
       k. Aristion
       l. Jude

B. Audience

   1. Believers from a Jewish background?

   2. Gentiles being tempted by a Judaized form of Christianity?

C. Setting: 2nd generation church flirting with apostasy.

D. "Brief" word of exhortation (13:22).

E. Finest Greek in the New Testament

F. Structure: based around seven Old Testament citations

   1. Psalm 48:4-6 (in Hebrews 2:5-18)

   2. Psalm 95:7-11 (in Hebrews 3:7-4:13)

   3. Psalm 110:4 (in Hebrews 4:16-7:28)

   4. Jeremiah 31:31-34 (in Hebrews 8:1-10:18)

   5. Habakkuk 2:3-4 (in Hebrews 10:32-12:3)

   6. Proverbs 3:30-31 (in Hebrews 12:4-13)

   7. [Exodus 19, Sinai] (in Hebrews 12:18-29)

G. Christology

   1. Sevenfold description of ministry of Christ (heir, role in

creation, radiance, representation, sustainer, purification, reign)

    2. Theme: The new covenant is superior to the old covenant. Jesus fulfills the Law. Therefore we will lose our salvation if we turn our backs on Jesus. Despite our sufferings, the fight is worth it. Do not give up!

H. Hebrews serves as a "bridge" book in the Bible, spanning the testaments.

III. Miscellaneous studies

A. Apostasy

    1. "Falling away" a technical term in the New Testament.

    2. Many verses warn of the possibility of losing one's salvation—*contra* the teaching of many Protestant groups.
       a. Hebrews was in fact declared an inferior document by Martin Luther because it rejects "once saved, always saved."
       b. There are at least a dozen verses which warn of the perils of apostasy: 2:1, 3:12, 3:19, 4:1, 4:11, 6:4-8, 6:12, 10:26-31, 12:15, 12:25-29.

B. Better covenant, better lifestyle—study of the two halves of Hebrews

    1. Superior covenant (1:1-10:18)

    2. Superior life (10:19-13:25)

C. The Old Testament sacrifices

    1. Some took place inside the Tabernacle/Temple

    2. Three special sacrifices took place outside the Temple
       a. Red Heifer (Numbers 19), Hebrews 9:3 [see The Red

Heifer Sacrifice at www.douglasjacoby.com]
- b. Scapegoat (Leviticus 16)
- c. Live bird (Leviticus 14)

3. Jesus fulfills them all in a very special way

D. Melchizedek

1. This righteous (and saved) individual was entirely "outside the system."
   a. Studying his role, and how it illustrates Jesus' own role, enables us to think "outside the box" and appreciate the deeper arguments the Hebrew writer uses to educate and enrich his readers.
   b. The writer is urging them not to be attracted to the old Jewish system. The case of Melchizedek furnishes evidence from within the Jewish Scriptures themselves in favor of the case for Christ.

2. About Melchizedek
   a. Genesis 14:18— Melchizedek was a figure greater than Abraham. (Abraham gave a tithe to him!)
   b. Melchizedek literally means King of justice rightness.
   c. Melchizedek was a very popular figure in contemporary Judaism.
   d. He had no genealogy. (Not necessarily to say that he was immortal, although some in popular Judaism interpreted him that way!)

3. The scriptural argument
   a. Psalm 100:4— Melchizedek was a priest not of the order of Aaron.
      i. That is, he was not descended from Judah, since he was completely outside the Jewish system thus making his priesthood a good analogy for that of Jesus Christ.
      ii. His order was superior to the Levitical priesthood.
   b. Hebrews 5-7 (various verses)

    i. Jesus' righteous priesthood (5:6-10)
    ii. Jesus' imperishable priesthood (6:20)
    iii. Jesus superior to Abraham (7:1-17)
  c. Melchizedek a model of godly living and kingship
    i. King of Sodom—possess land through might
    ii. King of Salem—possess land through faith.
    iii. The intrusion of Melchizedek into the Abraham account foreshadows a novel and unique intervention by God in human affairs, to take place two millennia later.

E. "Discipling"

  1. Discipled by one another—3:12.

  2. Discipled by the word of God—4:12.

  3. Discipled by ourselves—5:12.

  4. Discipled by Old Testament persons of faith—6:12.

  5. Discipled by God (experience)—12:12.

F. Four impossible things

  1. To bring back someone who has fallen away—6:4.
    a. Note: "fall away" in New Testament normally means to reach a state of such hardness of heart— see Proverbs 29:1—that no return is possible.
    b. The New Testament prefers terms like "drift away" [Hebrews 2:1] and "wander away" [James 5:19-20].)

  2. For God to lie—6:18

  3. For the blood of bulls and goats to take away sins—10:4

  4. To please God without faith—11:6

IV. Jewish Christianity and the end of a generation

A. Some see a "grace period" in 30-70 AD

B. Hebrews is written within a couple of years of the end of this 40-year period

  1. The Jewish War of 66-73 AD had quite possibly already started.

  2. The Jewish people had had nearly forty years to repent.

  3. The need for the people of God was to go *forward*, not to look *back*.

V. Conclusion

A. Hebrews is extremely appropriate for our "spiritual" generation.

  1. Written to 2nd generation Christians—So many of us are "second generation" believers.

  2. Suffering was wearing them down—As we suffer, so we too can suffer erosion of faith and stamina.

  3. The "old system" was beginning to look attractive again—Do we look back to "the old"?

  4. They were forgetting valuable lessons of faith (biblical figures, their own leaders, personal experience). Are we tempted to forget?

B. Read! Study other books on Hebrews, for example Neil Lightfoot, *Jesus Christ Today,* and William Barclay, *Hebrews* (in Daily Study Bible commentary series). Read and read deeply. Let no analogy, no allusion to the Old Testament slip by.

C. Remember, the word of God is "living and active"!

THE GENERAL LETTERS
The Epistles of James, Peter, John, and Jude

I. Introduction

A. General epistles: written to clusters of churches rather than to individual congregations.

1. 2 and 3 John are exceptions
   a. Written to individuals/individual house churches.
   b. Still, the cities to which these shorter letters were directed are unknown.

2. Also called "the Catholic epistles," from *katholikos*, meaning "general, universal."

3. Hebrews is similar to the general epistles, though it is not usually grouped with these letters.

B. Seven letters in all

1. Five written by apostles and two brothers of Jesus Christ.

2. They comprise 21 chapters of the 260 chapters in the New Testament.

II. The epistles

A. James

1. Written by brother of the Lord (Galatians 2:1-13, Acts 15), probably in the 40s

2. Jewish Christian audience/readership

3. Echoes of the Sermon on Mount and *Sirach*

4. Practice what you preach and live in harmony (charity, speech, business ethics)

B. 1 Peter

1. Written by Peter in early 60s.

2. Suffering (especially unjustly) is part of the Christian life

3. This is to walk in the footsteps of Jesus.

4. Suffering strains relationships.

5. It is worth it!

C. 2 Peter

1. Written by Peter, sometime shortly before his execution in 64 AD (1:14), to combat false teaching.

2. False teachers scorn authority and advocate libertinism

3. Safeguard: grow in the knowledge of God

4. Significant parallels with Jude. (One appears to be dependent on the other.)

5. Extremely colorful language!

D. 1 John

1. Written by John, any time from the 60s to the 90s.

2. Docetism (< *dokein,* to seem)

3. Sin v. ignorance: Docetic enlightenment lacks moral dimension

The Faith Unfurled

      4. Because God truly came in the flesh, believers truly can overcome sin and love one another.

E. 2 John

    1. Written by John, any time from the 60s to the 90s.

    2. "1 John in miniature"

    3. Warning letter to a house church about probably arrival of false teacher(s)

    4. Redrawing lines of fellowship

F. 3 John

    1. Written by John, any time from the 60s to the 90s.

    2. Diotrephes v. Demetrius

    3. Ego plays a significant role in ambition for leadership. Especially visible in fellowship and hospitality.

    4. "Pen and ink" (v.13)—about letters in the 1st century
       a. Length—2 and 3 John are typical
       b. Material—papyrus quite common
       c. Format—standard (greeting, wish for good health, body, farewell)
       d. Discoveries in late 19th century illustrate
       e. Literacy and writing
          i. Many literate people employed amanuenses. (An amanuensis was a professional letter writer.)
          ii. Literacy was more common in the first century than previously thought.
          ii. For an excellent read, try to get hold of Alan Millard's *Reading and Writing in the Time of Jesus* (Sheffield: Sheffield Academic Press, 2000).

G. Jude

   1. Written by Jude, the brother of Jesus (Matthew 13:55).

   2. Note: Jude comes from *Judas* (Ἰούδας), the Greek form of the Hebrew *Yehuda* (יְהוּדה), the name of the patriarch and son of Jacob. The alternate English name is Judah.

   3. Rejection of authority and license to sin

   4. Certain judgment will fall on those who live carelessly and influence others to do the same.

   5. Relation to 2 Peter: expansion or contraction?

   6. Extremely colorful language.

III. Conclusion

A. These letters are extremely practical

   1. Helped believers fight worldliness and compromise.

   2. Helped believers resist Gnosticism.

   3. Dealt with real issues; nothing "swept under the rug."

B. They lend themselves very well to scripture memory. E.g., why not memorize James or 1 Peter?

C. For more on the general letters, please see *The Letters of James, Peter, John, Jude—Life to the Full* (IP, 2006).

REVELATION
Understanding Apocalyptic Literature; The End of the World

I. General

A. Apocalypse ('αποκάλυψις) means "revelation"

B. Written by the apostle John

C. Written for the churches in Asia, of which seven are (symbolically) selected (Revelation 2-3)

D. Written in the time of Nero (54-68) or Domitian (81-96) or Vespasian (69-79)

E. Occasion: "The early Christians' refusal to participate in the cult of the emperor (who was acclaimed "lord" and "savior") was putting them on a collision course with the state; John saw prophetically that it would get worse before it got better and that the churches were poorly prepared for what was about to take place, so he writes both to warn and encourage them and to announce God's judgments against Rome" (Gordon Fee, *How to Read the Bible Book by Book,* 426).

II. Interpretation

A. Revelation is also called a "prophecy" (1:3; 22:7, 10, 18, 19)

   1. Biblical prophecy generally relates to the immediate future

   2. Revelation 1:3 and Daniel 8:26

B. Interpretation of apocalyptic
   1. Pictorial language
   2. Numerology
   3. Animals represent kingdoms and persons
   4. Reverse rules of interpretation
      a. Normal prose: take everything literally unless forced to do otherwise.
      b. Apocalyptic: take everything figuratively unless forced to do otherwise.
      c. Literal language—see following table

LITERAL LANGUAGE AND THE BIBLE
(Excerpted from *Genesis, Science & History,* 2004. Note: This section also appears in *Foundations for Faith: Old Testament Survey* in the section on Old Testament Apocalyptic.)

This table contains a short, but adequate, list of unambiguously non-literal passages. Take a moment to ponder (and enjoy) their meaning were they meant to be taken *literally*! If every passage in the Bible must be taken literally, then...

Old Testament examples

- Genesis 41:57—Australian Aborigines bought grain from Joseph.
- Numbers 26:64—Joshua and Caleb died in the wilderness. (Oops!—verse 65)
- Job 41:20—The crocodile (leviathan) breathes fire.
- Psalm 62:2—God is made of stone.
- Psalm 91:4—God has feathers.
- Song 4:1—Solomon's bride had birds in her head.
- Isaiah 34:9-10—Edom is *still* on fire; the smoke is visible in the Middle East today.
- Jeremiah 15:8—There will be more widows in Judah than humans on the planet!

New Testament examples

- Mark 11:23—You can command Everest to jump into the Bay of Bengal.
- Luke 2:37—Anna *never* left the temple. Never.
- John 11:9—The entire human population lives on the equator.
- Acts 2:5—The Japanese were present in Jerusalem at Pentecost.
- 1 Corinthians 15:31—Paul died over 12,000 times between his baptism (34 AD) and beheading (68 AD).
- Philippians 3:2—Dogs performed circumcisions in the first century.
- Colossians 1:23—By 60 AD, *every* human being (and insect) had heard the gospel.
- Jude 13—Godless men are made of salt water.
- Revelation 22:16—Jesus is made of wood. (Or is it burning hydrogen?)

You get the idea! Certainly the prose sections of the Bible are to be taken literally—apart, of course, from figures of speech. Yet, the Bible has many poetic sections which cannot and are not meant to be taken literally. For example, in the box above we noticed Psalm 91:4, which speaks of God's wings and feathers. I've met no one who takes this literally. In the same way, sections of the Bible, like the book of Revelation, which are full of figurative speech and symbolism, cannot reasonably be taken "literally." With this in mind, a better way to describe our approach to the Scriptures is to say that we take them "at face value" or "seriously." Nearly always, context shows us whether a passage is literal or figurative. Both genres are equally good vehicles for truth.

    C. Old Testament background and interpretation

        1. Over 250 allusions in 404 verses

        2. Draws on Old Testament apocalyptic genre (Isaiah, Ezekiel, Daniel, Zechariah, etc)

        3. Multiple strands and streams come together in Revelation.

D. Timetable approach is bankrupt (1 Thessalonians 5:1)

1. "Millennium"= Latin for *a thousand years*
   a. Millennialism
      i. Belief in thousand-year reign of Christ on earth
      ii. Also called *chiliasm*.
      iii. Speculation based on a single portion of scripture in Revelation 20.
   b. Amillennialism = no millennium
   c. Premillennialism = 2nd coming of Christ precedes the "millennium"
   d. Postmillennialism = 2nd coming of Christ follows "millennium"

2. Predictions of the last day
   a. About "the end"
      i. Punishment on a nation
      ii. End of history
      iii. Predictions?
   b. A word about the "rapture" and the "tribulation"

E. The message of the book

1. Careful! On coming into Revelation, feels like entering a foreign country! The popular books normally do no exegesis at all, jumping rather to hermeneutics!

2. There are five major views: Preterist, Idealist, Historical, Historicist, Futurist

3. Chapter 12 is the key to understanding the book of Revelation

4. Despite appearances to the contrary, the war has been won.

5. Salvation has already come.

6. But the end is "not yet." Things will get worse before they get better.

Recommended reading: Gordon Ferguson, *Revelation Revealed* (IP, 2010); Jim McGuiggan, *Revelation* (Fort Worth: Star, 1976); Douglas Jacoby, *Revelation* audio series (IP, 2006).

XIV
CONCLUSION
Unfurling the Faith!

I. Appreciate the New Testament genre by genre

　A.　Gospels

　B.　Acts

　C.　Letters

　D.　Apocalypse

II. Appreciate the New Testament on five levels

　A.　verse

　B.　chapter

　C.　book

　D.　testament

　E.　Scripture

III. Appreciate extrabiblical knowledge

　A.　Historical background

　B.　Geography

　C.　Helpful books (see chapter 22)

　D.　Be a reader!

IV. Unfurling the faith: metaphors

A. The faith is a glorious banner. Unfurl it!

   1. March we forth in the strength of God
         With the banner of Christ unfurled,
      That the light of the glorious gospel of truth
         May shine throughout the world;
      Fight we the fight with sorrow and sin,
         To set their captives free,
      That the earth may be filled with the glory of God
         As the waters cover the sea.
         – A. C. Ainger (1841-1919),
           God is Working His Purpose Out, v.4.

   2. We seemed to see our flag unfurled,
      Our champion waiting in his place
      For the last battle of the world,
      The Armageddon of the race.
         – John Greenleaf Whittier (1807–1892), *Rantoul*

B. Faith as a sail

   1. Let it down!

   2. And prepare for the voyage of a lifetime.

Supplementary Materials

NEW TESTAMENT READING TIPS
Getting the most out of your personal study

I. Getting the most out of the New Testament

A. Realize each book has distinct theme(s) and emphases.

B. Read paragraph by paragraph, not verse by verse.

C. Read book by book, and keep track of what you have read.

D. Use multiple Bible versions. Recommendations:
1. Barclay's version
2. English Standard Version
3. Holman Christian Standard Bible
5. International Standard Version
4. Jerusalem Bible
6. The Message
7. New American Bible
8. New American Standard Bible
9. New Century Bible
10. New English Bible
11. New English Translation
12. New International Version
13. New King James Version
14. New Living Translation
15. New Revised Standard Version
16. Phillips Modern English
17. Today's English Version
18. Tyndale's New Testament

II. Challenge

A. If you've never completed the New Testament, aim to do so!
   1. If you have just become a Christian, you can cover the 260 chapters of the New Testament easily in less than three months by reading three chapters a day.
   2. If you have already read the entire New Testament, why not read it through again in another version?

B. Give God your very best!

III. The New Testament book by book—some major themes

A. Matthew—The Kingdom of God, with Jesus Christ as Messiah and king in fulfillment of the O.T. prophecies.

B. Mark—Identity of Jesus a secret except to those to whom it has been revealed; discipleship means taking up our cross.

C. Luke—Jesus' ministry, undertaken through the power of the Spirit, is for all persons: the marginalized, the needy, the poor, women…

D. John—Discipleship means remaining in Jesus' word, loving one another, and bearing fruit, as the Spirit continues the ministry of Jesus. Note: all four gospels focus strongly on the death and resurrection of Jesus—the events of the "passion."

E. Acts—Good news of salvation for Jew and Gentile alike as the Spirit directs evangelism of. Vol. II. of Luke.

F. Romans—Jews and Gentiles must be unified as the people of God, which is possible only on the basis of grace.

G. 1 Corinthians—The crucified Messiah is the central message of the gospel.

H. 2 Corinthians—Christian ministry—and leadership—is servanthood.

I. Galatians—Salvation is through faith, not obsessing over the passé regulations of the Old Covenant, which pander to the flesh (as over against the Spirit).

J. Ephesians—The cosmic scope of the work of Christ, especially in his church, brings all the world together.

K. Philippians—With Christ as the key to all of life, we can joyfully persevere through suffering and grow in character.

L. Colossians— The supremacy and all-sufficiency of Christ, because of which religious regulations are seen to be powerless, unable to effect the ethical Christian life at the heart of the faith.

M. 1-2 Thessalonians—Holiness, suffering, and fellowship are just a few of the emphases of the apostle in these letters. Though the day of judgment is on the way for the persecutors of Christians, we must focus in such as faith, sexuality, and productive living.

N. 1-2 Timothy—Spiritual Christian leadership is vital for the order and progress of the church. Leaders must persevere till the end, just as Christ and Paul did, against sin, theological error, and temptations to compromise.

O. Titus—God's people, and especially leaders, must do what is good, and stand firm against the error of false teachers.

P. Philemon—In the gospel we can all be reconciled, and as a result we are to treat one another with grace and respect.

Q. Hebrews—Christ is completely superior to the Old Covenant, so why would anyone "fall away" (return to the old)?

R. James—True, living faith is borne out practically, in such areas as charity, speech, and business ethics.

S. 1 Peter—To follow in the footsteps of Jesus is to suffer, especially to suffer unjustly.

T. 2 Peter—Growth in the knowledge of God is the safeguard against the destructive errors of the false teachers.

U. 1-2 John—Because God truly came in the flesh, believers truly overcome sin and love one another.

V. 3 John—Ego plays a significant role in ambition for leadership, and is especially visible in fellowship and hospitality.

W. Jude—Certain judgment will fall on those who live carelessly and influence others to do the same.

X. Revelation—Despite appearances to the contrary, God is in absolute control of history, and will vanquish his enemies—sooner or later!

THE BIBLE IN A YEAR
A workable plan for reading the whole Bible

THROUGH THE BIBLE IN A YEAR

Jan	Feb	Mar	April	May	Jun
1-2 Pet Mark	1-3 Jn John	1-2 Cor Titus	1-2 Tim Phm	Luke	Acts
Prov Gen	Ecc Song Exod[1] Lev[2]	Isa Num[3]	Jer Lam Deut	Ezk[4] Jos[5] Judg Ruth	Dan[6] Hos 1-2 Sm

Jul	Aug	Sep	Oct	Nov	Dec
Gal Eph Phil	Col 1-2 Th	Rom Jas	Matt Jude	Heb Rev	*(grace)*
Joel Amos Obad Jon Mic Nah 1 Kings	Habk Zeph Hag Zech Mal 2 Kings	Esth Job Ps 1-50	Ezra Neh 1 Chr[7] Ps 51-100	2 Chr Ps 101-150	

Skimming suggestions (skim the portions indicated):

1: ch. 25-30, 35-40   3: ch.1-2, 7...   5: ch. 11-21   7: ch. 1-9
2: ch. 1-7   4: ch. 40-48   6: ch. 7-12

New Testament Suvey
Learn 100+ useful passages

Learn to locate the 100+ passages by chapter number only. There are many practical points from each chapter. Aim to begin using these passages a.s.a.p. in your counseling and evangelism!

Matthew
1.25	Mary's virginity (Catholicism)
6.15	Forgiveness in damaged relationships
6.33-34	Seeking first
7.7-8	Seeking and finding
7.13-14	Narrow road
13.55-56	Jesus' family (Catholicism)
22.29	Biblical ignorance
22:37-40	Greatest commandment(s)
23.9	Honorific titles ("Father")
28.19-20	Great Commission

Mark
1.16-20	Fishers of men
2.22	Fresh start (wineskins)
3.20-21	Family opposition
7.6-9	Traditions
7.20-23	Sin
11.24	Faith
16.16	Baptism

Luke
6.22-23, 26	Opposition
9.23-26, 9.57-62	Discipleship
10.38-42	Worry and distraction
13.1-5	Repentance
14.25-34	Counting the Cost
16.13	Two masters (see 14.26)
18.9-14	Self-righteousness

John
1.14	Incarnation
2.17	Jesus' zeal and conviction
8.31-32	Discipleship (word)
12.24	Death to self
12.47-50	Word
13.34-35	Discipleship (love)
15.8, 16	Discipleship (fruit)

Acts
2.6-11	Tongues = real languages
2.38	Conversion
2.42-47	The New Testament church
11.26	Disciples
17.10-12	Bereans
22.16	Baptism
24.25	Convenience
26.19-21	Repentance

Romans
1.18-32	Sin; the Fall
3.23-24	Sin
6.3-4	Baptism
6.23	Sin
8.9	Spirit
13.8	Debts

1 Corinthians
1.10-12	Factions (denominations)
4.3-4	Motives and conscience
5.12-13	Church discipline
6.9-11	Sin and change
6.20	Body is temple
7.15	Separation
7.39	Marrying a Christian

2 Corinthians
5.14	Christ's love compels us
6.14	Marrying a Christian
7.10-11	Repentance

The Faith Unfurled

Galatians
1.6-10 — False doctrine
3.26-27 — Baptism
5.19-21 — Sin
6.7-10 — Sowing and reaping

Ephesians
2.8-10 — Grace
2.19-22 — The church
5.3-7 — Sin

Philippians
1.21 — To live is Christ
4.13 — All things through Christ

Colossians
2.12 — Baptism
2.16-18 — Sabbath etc.
3.5 — Sin

1 Thessalonians
2.13 — Word
4.3 — Sexual sin
5.1 — End of world

2 Thessalonians
3.10 — Get a job!

1 Timothy
2.5 — One mediator
4.1-5 — Celibacy and food rules
4.16 — Word

2 Timothy
1.7 — Spirit
2.15 — Workman (the word)
2.23-26 — Patient instruction
3.1-5 — Sin
3.16-17 — The word
4.1-5 — Preach the word!

Titus
1.5-9 — Eldership (also 1 Timothy 3)
2.11 — Grace

Philemon (all) Leadership style

Hebrews
3.12-13	Church
4.12-13	Word
5.11-14	Spiritual maturity
10.23-25	Church
11.6	Faith
13.4	Extramarital sex
13.7, 17	Leadership/followership

James
1.19-21	Quick to listen
1.26	Control tongue
2.24	"Faith alone"?
4.17	Sins of omission
5.16	Confession

1 Peter
2.21-25	The Cross
3.1-7	Marriage
3.21	Baptism
4.3-4	Partying

2 Peter
1.3-11	Spiritual growth
1.16	Fact and fiction
2.1-3	False prophets
2.20-22	Returning to the world
3.16	Paul's scriptures

1 John
2.3-6	Obedience
2.15-17	Worldliness
4.20	Hatred and racism
5.13	Assurance of salvation

Revelation
3.16	Lukewarmness
3.20	Knocking at the door
21.8	Sin
22.18-19	Word

DATING
New Testament Chronology

I. General principles

A. The letters precede the gospels.

B. There are many points in secular history allowing us to cross-check biblical dates and events.

C. Shouldn't be too dogmatic *vis-à-vis* New Testament dating. There are radically different interpretations of the data, e.g. John A. T. Robinson, *Redating the New Testament* (Philadelphia: Westminster, 1976).

II. Dating the events in the life of Jesus Christ

A. Key passages: Luke 2:1ff, 3:1ff.

B. Birth—Herod the Great died 4 BC, thus any date after 6 BC is problematic.

C. Ministry—Tiberius Caesar reigned 14-37 AD. His 14th year would have covered 27/28 AD. Death of Herod Philip 34 AD, allowing two years only during which Passover fell on a Friday, 30 and 33. Jesus was "about 30" when he started his public ministry, and he worked (using John's chronology) for around three years.

D. Pilate was in Judea 26-36 AD. John the Baptist's ministry was over by 28 and Jesus' ministry had begun by 28 AD. If so, 33 is too late for Jesus' death. April 7, 30 AD would have been the Passover date marking Jesus' execution.

III. Dating events in the life of Paul

A. Conversion no later than 34 AD.
B. In Arabia and Damascus, 34-37 AD. First visit to Jerusalem, 37 AD.
C. First Missionary Journey, 48 AD.
D. Galatians written, 49 AD. Jerusalem Council, 49 AD.
E. Jews expelled from Rome by Claudius, 49 AD. Gallio in Corinth, 51 AD (inscription).
F. In Corinth, 50-52 AD. Writes 1-2 Thessalonians.
G. In prison (Caesarea), 57-59 AD.
H. Paul arrives in Rome (at the latest), 60 AD. Writes the 4 prison epistles. Released, 62 AD.
I. Re-arrested following events of July 64 AD (Great Fire of Rome), 64/65 AD.
J. Executed, 65-68 AD.

IV. Destruction of Jerusalem, 70 AD.

A. Key New Testament date.

B. Hebrews written before this time (Hebrews 8:13).

C. In my view, Revelation also (69 AD).

Key Dates to Remember

6 BC—birth of Christ
26 AD—Pilate to Judea
28 AD—public ministry of Christ begins, or perhaps in 27 AD.
30 AD—death and resurrection of Christ, start of the church of Christ
34 AD—conversion of Saul (Paul)
48 AD—First Missionary Journey
49 AD—Council of Jerusalem
62 AD—Paul released from Roman prison, further missionary work
64 AD—Great Fire of Rome, Christians blamed
70 AD—Destruction of Jerusalem. (See the article by that name at www.douglasjacoby.com.)

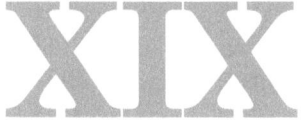

CANON
How the New Testament Came Together

I. *Kanon* (measuring rod, limits, sphere, area, principle, rule)

  A. Principles

    1. The genuine writings precede the false writings.

    2. Apostolicity
      a. Matthew – by apostle
      b. Mark – by companion of apostle Peter
      c. Luke-Acts – by companion of apostle Paul
      d. John, 1-3 John, Revelation – by apostle
      e. Romans-Philemon – by apostle
      f. Hebrews – by associate of apostle Paul
      g. James – brother of Jesus Christ (called apostle in Hebrews 3:1)
      h. 1-2 Peter – by apostle
      i. Jude – brother of Jesus Christ

    3. Recognition, not vote.
      a. New Testament came together under superintendence of the Holy Spirit
      b. No single person or group "decided" what should be in the Bible.

II. Development of Canon through time

  A. Documents written (1st century)

    1. Possibly several copies were immediately made of the originals.

    2. Use of secretaries was widespread. *Amanuensis* is the

technical term for the professional who wrote the letter at the speaker's dictation. Earliest canons are that of Marcion (140s) and also the Muratorian Canon (180).

B. Documents distributed (1st-2nd centuries)

1. There is no reason multiple copies could not be disseminated quickly throughout the Roman Empire.

2. Not all Christian communities would have necessarily ended up with the same documents.

C. Final form (27 documents) established by time of *Letter of Athanasius* (367 AD).

III. Conclusions

A. The New Testament canon was formed through the providence of God.

1. This took place through the inspiration and guidance of the Holy Spirit.

2. This can be seen as the fulfillment of Jesus' promise to the apostles in John 14:26 and 16:13.

B. The early church recognized the authority of these documents; they did vote on their inclusion in the canon.

C. The canon is complete and closed. No vacancy!

D. Further reading

1. Neil Lightfoot, *How We Got the Bible* (Grand Rapids: Baker, 1988)

2. Douglas Jacoby, *Compelling Evidence for God and the Bible* (Eugene: Harvest House, 2010)

3. _____, *How We Got the Bible* (IP, 2005), Audio

NEW TESTAMENT SURVEY CLASS SERIES
How to teach The Faith Unfurled as a church course

I. General principles

A. Although all the material may be helpful, not all the material need be taught in order to develop an interesting and helpful course.
B. Decide how many units to create depending on the number of available weeks and the interest level in the local church.
C. Be generous in your time allotment. If, for example, you have a 12-week window, plan on only 10 or 11 classes. Allow for interruptions to the church schedule.
D. Blend the supplementary information into the class sessions where appropriate.
E. If you are the teacher, make sure you yourself have studied all the lessons and supplementary material thoroughly. Also be sure to take the examination (advanced level).
F. Hold each class to around 30-35 minutes, and then allow time for questions.
G. It may be a good idea to encourage the class to read the New Testament during the course of the class. E.g., a 10-week class would span 64-70 days. At 4 chapters of the New Testament a day, students would be able to complete the New Testament during the length of the course.
H. If students have already finished the New Testament in one version, urge them to re-read it in another translation.
I. Strongly encourage new members to memorize the order of the books of the New Testament by the second session.

J. Show enthusiasm and others will likely respond with interest and willingness to challenge themselves.
K. Use the examinations (chapter 21). They can be taken in class or at home.

II. Teaching plans

A. Full 14 weeks
  1. Each of the first 13 chapters is a class.
  2. Final session is a review of materials and a charge based on chapter 14.
  3. Encourage the students to study the supplementary materials on their own, or to listen to the extra material in the audio series.

B. Expanded version
  1. Same as above but more weeks
  2. Allow a few extra classes to cover such issues as Canon, Chronology, Bible reading strategies, etc.

C. Short version—7 weeks
  1. Chapter 1 (overview). Skim through the handbook. Talk about expectations.
  2. Chapters 2 and 3 (Pax Romana and Jesus Christ)
  3. Chapters 4 and 5 (Synoptic Gospels and John). Encourage the class to read chapter 6 on their own (Contradictions).
  4. Chapter 7 (Acts)
  5. Chapters 8, 9, and 10 (Paul)
  6. Chapters 11 and 12 (Hebrews and General Letters)
  7. Chapters 13 and 14 (Revelation and Conclusion)

D. Audio possibilities
  1. Audio plan—listen to series on own time, meeting only to discuss and take the final exam.
  2. Hybrid plan—listen to some lessons on CD, meet for teaching of others

E. Advanced Plan
   1. Combine one of the plans above with extra work
      a. The 100 Useful Passages (chapter 17)
      b. Include extra reading or web surfing assignments from chapter 22
   2. This would be especially suitable if you are aiming to equip leaders, teachers, preachers…

F. When to teach the Survey
   1. A midweek series
   2. Sunday morning adult education (Sunday School)
   3. A series of special weekend sessions

III. Why a New Testament survey is important

A. Many Christians do not have the "big picture"! They do not see how the Bible fits together. New Testament (and O.T.) surveys are desperately needed.

B. Surveys take some of the "mystery" out of the Bible, building confidence and encouraging sharing of the material (counseling and evangelism)

C. Surveys help students to see how practical the Bible is.

D. *Without* a firm theological basis:
   1. People are at the mercy of others (relying on their interpretations rather than doing their own study).
   2. Bible reading easily becomes dull.
   3. Spiritual roots are shallow, not deep (Matthew 7:24-27).

E. *With* a firm theological basis:
   1. Roots are deeper and people look to the Scriptures for perspective, not just their friends.
   2. Bible reading becomes an adventure.
   3. *Competence* grows—and therefore…
   4. *Confidence* grows—and therefore…
   5. *Credibility* is enhanced. We are better able to make spiritual truths real to others.

NEW TESTAMENT EXAMS
At Introductory, Intermediate, and Intensive levels

"Test yourself"! (2 Corinthians 13:5)
Now that you have completed *The Faith Unfurled: New Testament Survey*, you may want to test your knowledge. Three different examinations have been prepared, and you will want to choose the one that best matches your knowledge level.

Three levels, three exams
The Introductory level examination is the one most students will choose, especially if they have been Christians only a few years, or if *The Faith Unfurled* is their first New Testament survey. The Intermediate level exam is more thorough, and assumes a broader knowledge of the Bible, while the Intensive examination is only for the stout of heart, and covers even more New Testament facts, verses, and issues not necessarily covered in the handbook or in audio lessons.

To prepare for the examinations
Be sure you know the order of the books of the New Testament. There will be short-answer or identification questions as well. Don't forget your N.T. geography, and the major historical characters. Also, be familiar with the flow of N.T. history.

In the Introductory and Intermediate examinations, no material found in the supplementary chapters (15-19) will be covered. The Intensive Examination, however, will include some material from the supplementary chapters. Aim to spend one or two hours preparing for the examination. The examination should take you no more than an hour to complete.

On your honor
These are closed-book examinations. Grade them—on your honor! (No, there is no answer key.) The maximum score on each test is 100 points.

Further exams
If you really enjoy Bible quizzes, you will find scores of interesting tests at **www.douglasjacoby.com**, including quizzes on various books of the Bible, alphabetic quizzes, "bullet tests," thematic tests, and much more. Good luck!

THE FAITH UNFURLED: NEW TESTAMENT SURVEY INTRODUCTORY LEVEL EXAM
No time limit

I. Order of New Testament books (20 points—2 points each)
Write the name of the book that follows the book given. Feel free to abbreviate.

1. Mark _____
2. 3 John _____
3. Acts _____
4. 2 Corinthians _____
5. Ephesians _____
6. Galatians _____
7. Hebrews _____
8. 2 Peter _____
9. John _____
10. Romans _____

II. Identifications (20 points—2 points each)
Explain briefly the significance of the following terms, events, persons, and dates. *A few words are sufficient.*

1. Augustus Caesar

2. 30 AD

3. 70 AD

4. Luke-Acts

5. Apocalypse

6. Pontius Pilate

7. Saul of Tarsus

8. Synoptic

9. 6 BC

10. Catholic Epistles

III. Short answer questions (20 points—5 points each)

1. Church leaders in the 4th century voted on which books should belong in the New Testament.   True or False?

2. Place the following names in order of *death*:
Jesus   Herod the Great   Peter   The Apostle James

3. Which was the *northernmost* of the three following regions?
JUDEA   SAMARIA   GALILEE

4. Name the transitional character between the testaments, also a powerful prophet of God.

IV. Geography (20 points—2 points for each feature)
Draw a map of the Roman Empire. Label the following:

Italy
Mediterranean Sea
Greece
Jerusalem
Israel
Red Sea
Rome
Egypt
Alexandria

V. Short essay (20 points—for writing a paragraph or two)
Write down what you have learned through studying this New Testament course. Has *The Faith Unfurled* strengthened your faith? (How?) What will be different in the future when you read the New Testament?

THE FAITH UNFURLED: NEW TESTAMENT SURVEY INTERMEDIATE LEVEL EXAM

Time limit: one hour.

I. Order of New Testament books (20 points)
Write out all the New Testament books in order. Subtract 2 points for any book omitted or out of order.

II. Short answer questions (20 points—5 points each)

1. Church leaders in the 4th century voted on which books should belong in the New Testament. True or False? Explain your answer.

2. Place the following names in order of *death*:
Jesus   Herod the Great   Peter   The Apostle James   John

3. Which was the *northernmost* of the three following regions?
JUDEA   SAMARIA   GALILEE   EGYPT

4. Why is the Pax Romana significant for Christians? Explain its meaning, and illustrate with facts.

III. Matching (40 points—2 points each)
Write the corresponding letter from the list at the right in the blank before the term on the left.

1. ____ Saul of Tarsus   A. "Roman peace"

2. ____ 66-73 AD   B. Revelation

3. ____ 25th N.T. book   C. Common language of the Empire

4. ____ Pastoral Epistles   D. The New Testament

5. ____ Anonymous letter   E. Fall of Jerusalem

6. ____ Apocalypse   F. The suffering of Christ

7. ____ Onesimus   G. Bound circumcision & Sabbath

8. ____ Synoptics   H. The Jewish War

9. ____ 70 AD   I. 1-2 Timothy and Titus

10. ____ Koine Greek   J. The Apostle Paul

11. ____ Pax Romana   K. Philemon's ex-slave

12. ____ 48 AD   L. Matthew, Mark, Luke

13. ____ Essenes   M. Persecuting emperor, 81-96 AD

14. ____ 260 chapters   N. One generation of church history

15. ____ Apocalyptic   O. Beginning of Christian church

16. ____ Judaizers   P. First Missionary Journey

17. ____ Passion   Q. Hebrews

18. ____ Domitian   R. Genre of Literature

19. ____ Acts   S. 3 John

20. ____ Pentecost   T. Gave up on "the system"

IV. Geography (10 points)
Draw a map of the Roman Empire. Label the following. (2 points off for each feature incorrectly labeled)

Italy
Mediterranean Sea
Greece
Jerusalem
Israel
Red Sea
Rome
Egypt
Alexandria

V. Short essay (10 points—for writing a paragraph or two)
Write down what you have learned through studying this New Testament course. Has *The Faith* Unfurled strengthened your faith? (How?) What will be different in the future when you read the New Testament?

THE FAITH UNFURLED: NEW TESTAMENT SURVEY INTENSIVE LEVEL EXAM

Time limit: one hour.

I. Order of New Testament books (10 points)
Write out all the New Testament books in order. Subtract 5 points for any book omitted or out of order.

II. Short answer questions (20 points–5 points each, no partial credit).

1. Selection, Arrangement, Adaption–explain how these principles relate to the writing of the Gospels.

2. Place the following New Testament documents in chronological order:

Revelation   James   Luke   Mark   Romans

3. Name three of the four principles comprising Paul's philosophy of missions.

4. Place the following N.T. events into chronological order:

Crucifixion	1. _____
3rd Missionary Journey	2. _____
Council at Jerusalem	3. _____
Nero persecutes Christians	4. _____
Pentecost	5. _____

III. Historical dates (20 points—2 points each)
Briefly, what is the significance of each of the following New Testament dates?

1. 27 BC

2. 6 BC

3. 26-36 AD

4. 27/28

5. 30 AD

6. 34 AD

7. 48 AD

8. 66-73

9. 70

10. 96

The Faith Unfurled

IV. Useful scriptures (20 points—2 points each)

1. _____ Matthew 13:55-56   A. Forgiveness in hurt relationships

2. _____ 2 Peter 2:1-3   B. Self-righteousness

3. _____ James 1:19-21   C. Baptism

4. _____ Titus 1:5-9   D. Celibacy and food rules

5. _____ 2 Timothy 3:16-17   E. Motives and conscience

6. _____ Luke 18:9-14   F. Tongues = real languages

7. _____ Matthew 6:15   G. The Greatest Commandment

8. _____ Luke 10:38-43   H. The Great Commission

9. _____ John 1:14   I. Hatred and racism

10. _____ 1 Corinthians 4:3-4 J. Quick to listen!

11. _____ Romans 13:8   K. False prophets

12. _____ Matthew 22:37-40   L. Elders

13. _____ Galatians 3:26-27   M. The word of God

14. _____ 1 Thessalonians 5   N. Marrying a Christian

15. _____ 1 Timothy 4:1-5   O. Stay out of debt!

16. _____ Acts 2:6-11   P. Jesus' brothers & sisters

17. _____ 1 John 4:20   Q. Worry and distraction

18. _____ 1 Corinthians 7:39   R. Incarnation

19. _____ Matthew 28:19-20   S. Sowing and reaping

20. _____ Galatians 6:7-9   T. The end of the world

V. Geography (10 points)
Draw a map of the Roman Empire. Label the following. (2 points off for each feature incorrectly labeled)

Italy
Mediterranean Sea
Greece
Jerusalem
Israel
Red Sea
Rome
Egypt
Alexandria

VI. Miscellaneous (10 points)

1. Which letter of the alphabet represents the theoretical common source both Matthew and Luke used in writing their gospels (in addition to Mark, "special M," and "special "?

2. Who was executed in Acts 7, and who presided over his execution?

3. Which goddess was worshipped in Ephesus?

4. How many chapters are there in Acts?

5. What is the shortest chapter of the New Testament?

6. Our modern versions are perfect translations of the original manuscripts. True or False?

7. Who were James, Joseph, Judas and Simon?

8. Who "rewrote" the New Testament omitting anything having to do with "the Old Testament god"?

9. In which century was the New Testament completed?
1st   2nd   3rd   4th

10. How many of Paul's letters are in the New Testament?

VII. Short essay (10 points—for writing a paragraph or two)
Write down what you have learned through studying this New Testament course. Has *The Faith Unfurled* strengthened your faith? (How?) What will be different in the future when you read the New Testament?

RESOURCES
Helpful Books and Websites

BOOKS

Barrett, C. K. *The New Testament Background: Selected Documents* (New York: Harper & Row, 1961).

Bivin, David, and Roy Blizzard Jr. *Understanding the Difficult Words of Jesus: New Insights From a Hebrew Perspective,* 1994.

Black, Matthew. *An Aramaic Approach to the Gospels and Acts,* 1998.

Brauch, Manfred T., *Hard Sayings of Paul* (Downers Grove: Intervarsity, 1989)—handy "difficult passages" volume.

Bruce, F. F., *Hard Sayings of Jesus* (Downers Grove, Intervarsity Press, 1983)—another handy "difficult passages" volume.

Bruce, F. F. *Paul Apostle of the Heart Set Free.* (Grand Rapids: Eerdmans, 2000).

____, *Jesus and Christian Origins Outside the New Testament* (Toronto: Hodder & Stoughton, 1984)—well worth reading, if you can get hold of an old copy.

Carson, D. A., *Exegetical Fallacies* (Grand Rapids: Baker, 1996)—technical, but excellent; best for those over 10 years in the faith, and important reading for all who studied Classical or Koine Greek.

____, *New Testament Commentary Survey* (Grand Rapids: Baker, 1993)—an invaluable tool if you are in the market for a commentary or commentary series.

Davids, Peter H., *More Hard Sayings of the New Testament* (Downers Grove, Intervarsity, 1991).

Deissmann, Adolf, and Lionel Richard Mortimer Strachan. *Light from the Ancient East; the New Testament Illustrated by Recently Discovered Rexts of the Graeco-Roman World,* 2012.

Drane, John, *Introducing the New Testament* (Oxford: Lynx, 1986)—a very readable survey.

Elwell, Walter A. and Robert W. Yarbrough. *Encountering the New Testament: A Historical and Theological Survey* (Encountering Biblical Studies). Grand Rapids: Baker, 2005.

Edersheim, Alfred. *The Life and Times of Jesus the Messiah: New Updated Edition.* Peabody, Mass.: Hendrickson, 1993.

Fee, Gordon D, *New Testament Exegesis: A Handbook for Students and Pastors* (Louisville: Westminster John Knox Press, 2002)—very technical.

Fee, Gordon & Douglas Stuart, *How To Read the Bible for All Its Worth* (Grand Rapids: Zondervan, 1993)—essential reading for anyone who has been reading the scriptures longer than five years.

Fee, Gordon D. & Douglas Stuart, *How to Read the Bible Book by Book: A Guided Tour* (Grand Rapids: Zondervan, 2002)—very useful overview.

Ferguson, Gordon. *Romans: The Heart Set Free.* Spring, Texas: IP, 2000.

Ferguson, Gordon, *Revelation Revealed* (Spring, TX: IP, 2011)—good introductory volume to the Apocalypse.

_____, *World Changers—The History of the Church in the Book of Acts* (Spring, TX: IP, 2011)—helpful.

Fitzmyer, Joseph A. *The Semitic Background of the New Testament* (Biblical Resource Series). Grand Rapids: Eerdmans, 1997.

Gundry, Robert. *A Survey of the New Testament.* (Grand Rapids: Zondervan, 2003).

Guthrie, Donald, *New Testament Introduction* (Downers Grove: Intervarsity, 1970)—long but excellent survey.

Jacoby, Douglas, *Foundations for Faith: Old Testament Survey* (Spring, TX: IP, 2004). Lays the O.T. foundation for N.T. appreciation.

_____, *The Letters of James, Peter, John, Jude—Life to the Full* (Spring, TX: IP, 2006)—on the epistles of James, Peter, John, and Jude. Easy to read.

Jeffers, James S. *The Greco-Roman World of the New Testament Era: Exploring the Background of Early Christianity,* 1999.

Josephus, Flavius. *The Works of Josephus: Complete and Unabridged, New Updated Edition.* Peabody, Mass.: Hendrickson, 1980.

Keener, Craig S., *The IVP Bible Background Commentary: New Testament* (Downers Grove: Intervarsity, 1993)—provides cultural background for many N.T. verses.

Kinnard, G. Steve, *Getting the Most from the Bible—Second Edition* (Spring, TX: IP, 2012)—focuses more on N.T. than O.T.

Kinnard, Steve G. *Prophets: The Voices of Yahweh.* (Billerica, Mass: Discipleship Publications International, 2001).

Lightfoot, Neil, *Jesus Christ Today: A Commentary on the Book of Hebrews* (Grand Rapids: Baker, 1989).

McBirnie, William Stewart. *The Search for the Twelve Apostles,* 1994.

McGuiggan, Jim, *Revelation* (Fort Worth: Star Bible Publications, 1976)—compelling, even if somewhat rambling in writing style.

_____, *The Book of Romans* (Looking into the Bible Series), 1982.

Metzger, Bruce M, *The Text of the New Testament: Its Transmission, Corruption, and Restoration* (New York: Oxford University Press, 1992).

Oakes, John, *From Shadow to Reality* (Spring, TX: IP, 2005). Able explanation of the prophecies, foreshadows, and typology connecting the two testaments.

Powell, Mark Allan. *Introducing the New Testament: A Historical, Literary, and Theological Survey,* 2009.

Schreiner, Thomas R. *Paul, Apostle of God's Glory in Christ: A Pauline Theology,* 2006.

Tenney, Merrill, *New Testament Survey* (Grand Rapids:Eerdmans, 1992).

Vine, W. E., Merrill F. Unger, and William White, Jr., *Vine's Complete Expository Dictionary of Old and New Testament Words* (New York: Thomas Nelson, 1985).

Witherington III, Ben, *The Paul Quest: The Renewed Search for the Jew of Tarsus* (Downers Grove: Intervarsity Press, 1998)—one of the best books on Paul out there.

Wright, N. T., *What Saint Paul Really Said: Was Paul of Tarsus the Real Founder of Christianity?* (Oxford: Lion, 1997)—superb refutation of liberal theological notions , well reasoned.

_____, *Who Was Jesus?* (London: S.P.C.K., 1992)—another superb book on the conservative side.

Yancey, Philip, *The Bible Jesus Read* (Grand Rapids: Zondervan, 1999). As usual, Yancey connects extremely well, making it easy to experience something of the first century atmosphere as your faith is illuminated.

WEBSITES

http://camellia.shc.edu/theology/NewTestament.htm
Bibliography: General works on the New Testament

http://cc.christiancourses.com/fs_bible-courses.php
ChristianCourses.Com

http://cc.christiancourses.com/fs_bible-courses.php
Christianity Today

http://home.rochester.rr.com/gocek/images/christn/
Christian symbols and glossary

http://journals.cambridge.org/bin/bladerunner?30REQEVENT=
&REQAUTH=0&500002REQSUB=&REQSTR1=NewTestament
Studies Cambridge Journals Online

http://members.aol.com/FLJOSEPHUS/ntparallels.htm
New Testament Parallels to the Works of Josephus

http://myweb.lmu.edu/fjust/bible.htm
Electronic New Testament Educational Resources

http://nestlealand.uni-muenster.de/
Greek New Testament manuscripts—University of Münster

http://philologos.org/__eb-jl/
Lightfoot New Testament Commentary

http://www.abu.nb.ca/courses/NTIntro/IndexNTIntr.htm
New Testament and Context (Atlantic Baptist University)

http://www.askelm.com/
Associates for Scriptural Knowledge

http://www.asor.org/
American Schools of Oriental Research

http://www.bib-arch.org/
Biblical Archaeology Society

http://www.bibleinterp.com/
The Bible and Interpretation

http://bible.crosswalk.com/Lexicons/Greek/
Crosswalk—New Testament Greek Lexicon

http://www.bible.org/
Trustworthy Bible Study Resources

http://www.bible-researcher.com/versions.html
English Versions of the Bible

http://www.biblicalhebrew.com/nt/hebrewgospel.htm
Matthew's Hebrew Gospel

http://www.biblicaltraining.com/class.php?class=NT203
Biblical Training

http://www.ccel.org/fathers2/
The Early Church Fathers

http://www.christianbook.com/
Christian Book Distributors

http://www.christianitytoday.com/ct/2003/138/21.0.html
Top Ten New Testament Archaeological Finds of the Past 150 Years

http://www.cin.org/users/james/files/deutero3.htm
Deuterocanonical references in the New Testament

http://www.doesgodexist.org/
Does God Exist?

http://www.douglasjacoby.com/
International Teaching Ministry of Douglas Jacoby

http://www.historicmint.com/coinsbible4B.html
Coins of the Bible

http://www.ibs.org/bibles/translations/index.php
International Bible Society

http://www.ipibooks.com
Illumination Publishers International

http://www.jimmcguiggan.com/
Jim McGuiggan

http://www.kchanson.com/papyri.html
New Testament Papyri and Codices

http://www.kingdavid8.com/Contradictions/Home.html
A Christian Look at Bible Contradictions

http://www.lasalle.edu/~dolan/nt.html
New Testament Links

http://www.library.yale.edu/div/ntbi.htm
Yale Bibliographic Introduction to the New Testament

http://www.menfak.no/bibel/vines.html
Vine's Expository Dictionary of New Testament Words

http://www.ntcanon.org/
Development of New Testament Canon

http://www.ntgateway.com/
The New Testament Gateway

http://www.ntgreek.net/
New Testament Greek

http://www.reasons.org/index.shtml
Reasons to Believe

http://www.roman-emperors.org/impindex.htm
Online Encyclopedia of Roman Emperors

http://www.scrollpublishing.com/
Scroll Publishing

http://www.searchgodsword.org/
Search God's Word (Abilene Christian University)

http://www.soniclight.com/constable/notes.htm
Dr. Constable's Bible Study Notes

http://www.teachmethebible.org/home/
Teach Me The Bible

http://www.theologywebsite.com/nt/
Theology Website and New Testament Helps

http://www.tyndale.cam.ac.uk/Tyndale/staff/Head/NT&Pap.htm
New Testament and Papyrology

http://www.worldinvisible.com/library/ffbruce/ntdocrli/ntdocont.htm
F.F. Bruce—*The New Testament Documents: Are They Reliable?*

Books by Douglas Jacoby

A Quick Overview of the Bible

Answering Skeptics

Campus Core

Chariots of Fire

Compelling Evidence for God and the Bible

Exodus: Night of Redemption

Foundations for Faith: Old Testament Survey

Jesus and Islam

Life to the Full

Principle-Centered Parenting

The Faith Unfurled: New Testament Survey

The Lion Has Roared

The Spirit

The Ultimate Bible Quiz Book

Thrive! Using Psalms to Help You Flourish

What Happens After We Die?

What's the Truth About Heaven and Hell?

El Espíritu

La Aljaba

www.ingramcontent.com/pod-product-compliance
Lightning Source LLC
Chambersburg PA
CBHW031426290426
44110CB00011B/538